Professionalism in Teaching

Second Edition

Beth Hurst
Southwest Missouri State University

Ginny Reding
Willard High School

Upper Saddle River, New Jersey
Columbus, Ohio

10 9 8 7 6 5 4 3 2 1

ISBN: 0-13-170550-4

NEW TO THIS EDITION

With increasing demands being placed on teachers, those new to the profession need an understanding of what it truly means to be a professional. They need to enter their classrooms armed with the necessary skills to face those demands with aplomb and confidence. The purpose of this supplemental, nuts-and-bolts book is to provide new teachers with practical, yet theory-based approaches to becoming the professional teachers they dream of being. New to this edition:

- New and updated "Advice from Professionals"

- Quotes from teachers interspersed throughout the text

- New and updated citations from the literature

- New and updated information on professional development

- New sections including:

  Becoming a Professional
  Professional Classroom Environment
  Reflective Decision-Making
  Mentoring
  Accountability
  Technology
  When a Parent Is Uninvolved
  Lifelong Learning
  Contributing to the Community of Learners
  Professional Teaching Portfolios
  Teachers' ABC's of Professionalism

- Updated Internet links to web sites divided into the following sections:
  Professional Education Organizations
  Professional Organizations for Teachers by Subject Area
  Related Educational Links for Teachers
  Teacher Accreditation, Accountability, and Standards
  Teacher Recruitment

- Updated appendices

TABLE OF CONTENTS

INTRODUCTION

*W*hy do some people seem to find teaching jobs quickly and easily while others appear to struggle in their efforts to get hired by a school system? What is it that causes principals to be eager to hire some and not others? What is the difference among job applicants who all attended the same university and sat through the same education courses? Why do some teachers drift from job to job, unable to stay in one place long enough to become tenured? The difference is simple, but is often simply overlooked: those who succeed have learned to present themselves as professionals. They have learned the rules for getting along with people—they have good social skills. Social skills can, and do, make all the difference in career success.

The inability to get along with others causes more people to lose their jobs than does job incompetence. This is true in the teaching profession as well as in other careers. In an age when teachers do not automatically have as much respect from the public as they did in previous generations, it is even more important that they have the necessary skills to deal appropriately with students, parents, colleagues, and administrators. Teachers will be more successful when they understand society's expectations of professionalism.

Many of the topics addressed in this book may seem like simple rules of social etiquette that most people know; however, this is an area in which many new teachers seem to be lacking. This book's purpose is to help you learn ways to be your best in the classroom, with parents, administrators, and the public, in order to help you be the successful, professional teacher you have dreamed of becoming.

ACKNOWLEDGMENTS

*S*pecial thanks to the following teachers and principals: Monica Andrews, Renee Bass, Patsy Bowser, Barbara Carnagey, Jamie Combs, Kate Companik, Gina Cowin, Kerri Cox, Russell Cox, Joyce Crumpley, Shannon Cuff, Cindy Delcour, Lori Elliott, Candace Fisk, Les Ford, Stephanie Hawn, Yvonne Heath, Janice Hogan, Deana Glasgow, Justine Lines, Jana Loge, Nelwyn Mathews, Janelle McBroom, Carol Plumley, Maria San Paolo, Christine Santhuff, Emmett Sawyer, Lori Spiegel, Faye Sturhahn, Todd Varhalla, and Randall Wallace.

PART ONE

PROFESSIONALISM AT ITS BEST

"Professionals possess expert knowledge, but often confront unique, problematic situations that do not lend themselves to formulaic solutions. Professionals must cultivate the ability to cope with the unexpected and act wisely in the face of uncertainty" (National Board for Professional Teaching Standards, 2004).

A good way to learn what it means to be a professional is to emulate those teachers whom you would label professional. Think about your professors in college. What characteristics do those who act in a professional manner exhibit? They most likely respect their students and treat them all fairly; they don't talk about other teachers or make derogatory statements in class about others; they do their best and expect your best; they understand the expectations of their job description and follow through with them; they find and bring out your best; and they have learned the appropriate social skills for our society.

The National Board for Professional Teaching Standards (2004) has set five propositions they believe make up a professional teacher. Those five propositions are:

1) Teachers are committed to students and their learning.
2) Teachers know the subjects they teach and how to teach those subjects to students.
3) Teachers are responsible for managing and monitoring student learning.
4) Teachers think systematically about their practice and learn from experience.
5) Teachers are members of learning communities. (NBPTS)

Everything you do as a teacher fits into one of these categories. Being a professional means making a conscientious effort to work at every aspect of teaching and setting high standards for yourself and your students. According to Lawson (2004), "Teachers are the educational leaders who have the greatest direct impact upon students; thus they are the most influential factors in stimulating and motivating students to greater achievement" (p. 2).

PROFESSIONALISM DEFINED

"Getting the job done, even done well, is good enough for nonprofessionals, but continually improving the way the job is done both for themselves and others is the hallmark of professionals" (Glasser, 1993, p. 12).

The noun *professional* means "a person who does something with great skill." That sounds nice, doesn't it? That's what you are—you are a professional. You have been trained for years and have earned, or soon will earn, a college degree. You have a great skill. The adjective *professional* means "worthy of the high standards of a profession." If you want people to see you as a professional, you want to learn what those high standards are for teachers, and then strive to meet them. The standards expected of teachers are what this book is all about.

William Glasser, M.D., author of the book *The Quality School Teacher*, believes that "professionals not only know how to do the job they are hired to do, but they are also given an opportunity to do that job the way they believe is best" (1993, p. 11). This is an apt description of teachers. Teachers are given a curriculum they are expected to teach, but they are usually given freedom, within limits, in how they actually convey that information to their students. You may be a gifted lecturer who enjoys dispensing information to students or you may be one who enjoys social interaction in your classroom and finds ways for students to work in pairs or in groups. One of the great joys of being a teacher is the freedom to find your own teaching style.

Teachers, as professionals, are always looking for better ways to do their job. That's what they find exciting about teaching. They like what they do. They care deeply about doing the best job they can to teach their students. You know this. It's probably why you became a teacher in the first place—you want to make a difference in the lives of students.

BECOMING A PROFESSIONAL

"To be a professional, you must look *the part,* act *the part, and* become *the part."*

—Maria San Paolo, Teacher

*D*o you remember the Skin Horse from Margery Williams' *The Velveteen Rabbit?* In the passage where he shares with the Rabbit the intricacies of becoming real, he says,

> You become. It takes a long time. That's why it doesn't often happen to people who break easily, or have sharp edges, or who have to be carefully kept. Generally, by the time you are Real, most of your hair has been loved off, and your eyes drop out and you get loose in the joint and very shabby. But these things don't matter at all, because once you are Real you can't be ugly, except to people who don't understand. (p. 17)

"Real" educators are those who make choices, often difficult choices, to be the best they can be. Students expect, and rightly so, that their teachers be genuine. Teachers are professionals and should consider themselves such; however, being labeled a professional does not automatically cause one to act professionally, and unfortunately, too many do not act the part. Becoming "real" is work. It's calculated effort and a focused mindset. Do you want to *become* a professional? Focus. Be deliberate—deliberate in your conduct, your planning, your communication, your relationships, your appearance, and obviously, your teaching.

PROFESSIONAL CLASSROOM ENVIRONMENT

"In addition to being knowledgeable in their subject, teachers must have the ability to communicate, inspire trust and confidence, and motivate students, as well as understand the students' educational and emotional needs" (Bureau of Labor Statistics, 2004).

*S*tudents respond to their environment. As the teacher, it is within your power to set the tone for your classroom. Your classroom will take on your personality, but with that comes a responsibility to be

11

professional in all you do. For example, there is nothing wrong with filing and polishing your fingernails; there *is* something wrong with doing it in the classroom while you are responsible for student learning. Expecting your students to be on task is important; just as important is your own focus. A teacher may try so hard to relate to the students that he uses poor judgment in making choices. For example, one who talks with students about partying over the weekend or who uses inappropriate language with students may win the "bonding" battle, but in the long run, will probably lose the war.

You only have to read the paper or listen to the news to hear of educators not only losing their jobs, but also being prosecuted because of foolish decisions and inappropriate behaviors with students. Improper conduct, including sexual activity or coarse talk, immediately takes a teacher out of the professional arena and into dangerous territory. Too much is at stake in the education of your students and your own career to jeopardize it by acting unprofessionally. If you're not certain whether or not something you say or do is appropriate, err on the side of being too careful rather than not careful enough. Unfortunately, it is not rare to hear of teachers who lose their jobs because they have failed to establish a professional environment.

Creating a professional classroom environment also includes making your classroom a safe place for students to explore new ideas and learn about new cultures. The National Board for Professional Teaching Standards (2004) states,

> The cultural diversity represented in many communities can serve as a powerful resource in teaching about other cultures, in encouraging tolerance and understanding of human differences, and in promoting civic ideals. Accomplished teachers seek to capitalize on these opportunities and to respond productively to students' diverse backgrounds.

Create the culture in your classroom to embrace the cultures of everyone in it.

REFLECTIVE DECISION-MAKING

"Teachers who reflect on yesterday make better decisions tomorrow."
—Janelle McBroom, Teacher

As a teacher you will be required to make countless decisions in your classroom. Sometimes you have time to think through your decisions and to consult with your mentor or administrator, but more often you must make decisions on the spot. In either case, your decisions should be based on sound judgment and your knowledge of good educational practice. Being a reflective decision-maker means stopping to think about and reflecting upon what you know and making deliberate, thoughtful decisions based on that knowledge. Perrone (1991) defines this reflection as "weighing issues and ideas, examining something from many different angles through a multiplicity of lenses, working through many options" (p. 23). Your professional training as a teacher has provided you with these "lenses." Stop and think first; then follow your professional training and your instincts.

Not only do you need to reflect before making decisions, but you also need to be reflective when setting goals for yourself and your students. Posner and Rudnitsky (1994) state, "As a teacher, you should always be thoughtful about your work, able to articulate your goals and to justify the time and resources spent striving for those goals" (pp. 53-54). Be thoughtful and deliberate when tying your lessons to objectives, aligning assessment with standards, and creating a classroom where students learn, grow, and thrive.

MENTORING

"With an experienced mentor providing support and assistance, the beginning teacher may refine his or her instructional skills, feel more successful, and ultimately choose to remain in the classroom" (Carver, 2004, p. 58).

Much has been written about how to mentor new teachers, but it is equally important that new teachers know how to be mentored. As a new teacher, you should be open and willing to be mentored. Often new teachers enter their classrooms with fresh ideas and enthusiasm from their college experiences. Sometimes they enter their new

13

schools with a desire to "change the world." While this zeal to make changes may indicate strong character, you should be cautious of pushing your agenda too quickly or stubbornly, and you should be careful not to come on too strong in efforts to change other teachers. Those teachers may be very happy with the way they are teaching and may not want to change. The following saying can be applied to this situation.

> *Try to change the world, and the world will destroy you;*
> *Change yourself, and the world around you changes.*
> —Author unknown

Rather than entering a school determined to change the educational system, work within the system and make changes in your own teaching. In a later section in this book, "Advice from Professionals," Principal Randall Wallace tells of a new teacher who refused to follow the curriculum in the school in which she was hired because she had different philosophical views than the administration. Rather than changing the school as she had hoped, she was not rehired the next year. Dr. Wallace suggests that following the established curriculum and supplementing it with her own ideas would have been a better and more productive approach. Then perhaps other teachers might have seen her ideas and sought her advice about implementing them in their own classrooms. This teacher was counseled about how to handle the situation, but she did not heed the advice, and as a result her contract was not renewed.

Don't be afraid that you are "bothering" your mentor when you go to him or her for advice. One of the great things about the nature of mentoring is that it is a two-way street. When mentors help others, they find they are being helped in return. According to Wesley (2003), "When veterans and novices work together in a nurturing relationship, each gets something of real value from the other. Veterans gain energy; novices gain inspiration" (p. 470). So don't hesitate to ask for help. Your mentor will benefit from it, too.

A mentor's purpose is to help you become acclimated in your new role as a teacher. Listen to what your mentor says, and be aware of opportunities to develop and mature as a teacher. Consider the following suggestions as ways to be successful in the mentoring process.

- *Seek out your mentor* when you have questions or problems instead of waiting for a scheduled meeting. A good mentor will appreciate being asked questions.

- *Seek out advice* not only from your assigned mentor, but also from other teachers you admire.

- *Ask your mentor to visit your classroom* some time during the first part of the year to offer suggestions on your classroom management or teaching styles.

- *Ask your mentor to look at a particular lesson plan* or your lesson plan book to see if your objectives are on track with your school's expectations.

- *Show respect for veteran teachers.* They have been teaching a long time and have much to offer. Listen to them. Heed their advice.

- *Don't forget to show appreciation* to your mentor for the help and advice you receive. A short note of thanks or even a box of chocolates is a thoughtful gesture of appreciation.

ACCOUNTABILITY

"Professional practice requires that teachers be knowledgeable about their legal obligation to carry out public policy as represented by state statute and regulation, school board directives, court decisions and other policies" (National Board for Professional Teaching Standards, 2004).

The word "accountability" has been used so often in recent years that teachers may cringe when they hear the word. In this age of high stakes testing, teacher certification tests, and standards for everything and everybody, teachers carry an additional responsibility of staying current with the ever-changing roles these issues play in education.

With the arrival of No Child Left Behind (NCLB), teachers are being held accountable for their students' success by so-called high stakes tests. These tests are generally standardized tests that determine whether or not students are promoted to the next grade level. Being required to meet specific standards does not have to mean you are not allowed some freedom in teaching. Lee (2003) believes "many content standards in state curricula can be embedded in sustained projects and other activities...and can be included in activities that provide meaningful contexts and purposes" (p. 454). Know what specific content you are required to teach in your grade level or subject area; know the standards that need to be met; and plan accordingly.

Accountability is not only about being able to show what your students know; it is also about being able to show your abilities as a teacher. Teachers must meet strict certification requirements through higher ACT/SAT scores for admittance into some teacher education programs and through certification tests such as PRAXIS, TexES in Texas, and C-SET in California. Other organizations have standards for teacher professionalism such as the Interstate New Teacher Assessment and Support Consortium (INTASC) and the National Board for Professional Teaching Standards (NBPTS). The INTASC (2004) standards "reflect the requisite knowledge, skills, and attitudes necessary for teachers starting their career."

TECHNOLOGY

"Workplace literacy requires the ability to access, interpret, compare and contrast, synthesize, and communicate ideas electronically" (Watts-Taffe, Gwinn, Johnson, & Horn, 2003, p. 130).

Keeping up to date with current advancements in technology is ongoing. More school systems are creating district and school web sites than ever before, and many teachers are joining in by providing their own classroom web sites. This not only adds excitement for students in the classroom, but it is beneficial for parents who are seeking information such as scheduling, assignments, upcoming events and activities, and faculty and administrative contacts. Having your own web page can be a wonderful asset for communication with students, parents, and administrators.

Some school systems provide a coordinator who oversees the technology program and educates teachers in methods of using the computer and other technology to enhance their teaching. Workshops and conferences are regularly provided for teachers who are interested in broadening their horizons in the area of technology.

We are more and more becoming a paperless society. In many schools, teachers are required to report attendance as well as grades on the computer. They may be asked to use programs that figure class grades, provide seating charts, record parent information, give student scheduling information, and offer many other features. A word of warning: teachers must be sensitive to the significance of having all of this information at their fingertips. Administrators may suggest that teachers do not refer to students by their full names in email so that students' privacy will not be violated. A teacher should also be consistent in not allowing students to have access to the computer that houses sensitive information. A student who gets into a teacher's computer and manipulates the system or gathers private information can do much damage. A professional realizes the responsibility of having access to this information and is cautious about giving others opportunities to access it.

State departments and school systems are always looking toward the future and working to prepare their students to be successful in a world of technology. You may become a part of a school system that is on the cutting edge of technological instruction, and you may be asked to be a part of it. One such program that began a few years ago is the state of Missouri's eMINTS (enhancing Missouri's Instructional Networked Teaching Strategies). The state department selects school districts, which in turn select classrooms (usually third or fourth grade) to participate in the program. The purpose of eMINTS is to "support Missouri educators as they integrate multimedia technology into inquiry-based, student-centered, interdisciplinary, collaborative teaching practices" (Reding, 2002, p. 23). Teachers involved in the program undergo rigorous training to learn how to use the wide variety of technology provided for their students, which includes a high-speed Internet connection, SMART Board, high-lumen projector, a computer for every two children, and a digital camera, among other things. One teacher in an eMINTS classroom, Rhonda Glaser, says, "What you get out of this is what you put in it. You must be willing to change" (Reding, p. 24). She finds it very exciting to observe the technological learning of her students. She states, "We all talk about moving toward the teacher as being facilitator. An 'aha' moment for me was when we had three things that needed to be done by the end of the day. I stood back and realized that my students had become self-sufficient. They were able to work on their own as I facilitated. I stood back and watched self-sufficient learning" (p. 24).

Being a professional requires one to be proactive in the area of technology. Whether or not your district provides you with the latest technology and the mandate to use it, your responsibility as a teacher is to do your best to provide your students with opportunities to grow. The continuing advancement in technology is certainly one way our society is changing on a daily basis, and it provides you with the challenges and opportunities for growing along with it.

EFFECTIVE SOCIAL SKILLS

"Good teachers know that teaching is a 'people profession' and understand that how they present themselves in the classroom will go a long way in motivating their students to learn."

—Candace Fisk, Teacher

Social skills are much like the "rules" of professionalism. Some people use the term "people skills," but whatever the term, the meaning is the same. Knowing how to conduct oneself in the presence of people is a learned skill. As Robert Fulghum reminds us in *All I Really Need to Know I Learned in Kindergarten*, these are skills we should have learned early in life. Notice the students in classrooms who have the most trouble—those who spend more time in the principal's office than out of it. Generally speaking, these are the students who haven't learned how to get along with others. Teachers who lack social skills are also asking for trouble. Practicing good social skills is a great start toward becoming a professional.

Faux Pas

"Being a little awkward or naïve can be charming. Thinking you know it all is unforgivable" (Toth, 1999).

A faux pas is a social blunder, an error in etiquette, or a tactless act or remark. A faux pas can cost you a teaching job. Make one in an interview and you might find yourself out of the running. Make too many while teaching, and you might find yourself not invited back next year. These are not exaggerations. More teachers lose their jobs because of problems with professionalism and social skills than for any other reason.

Below is a list of questions regarding social skills. You may have already considered these, but seeing them again may help to serve as a reminder of their importance. If you are unsure of how you measure up in some of these areas, ask a kind friend to review the list with you to help you evaluate yourself more clearly. Read the following checklist to see how well you practice these social skills.

- *Do you talk too much?* A person who talks incessantly quickly loses his audience and perhaps even his validity. People quickly tire of someone who goes on and on without allowing others the opportunity to contribute. If you are talking and get interrupted, wait a minute or so to see if anyone comes back to ask you what you were saying. If not, re-evaluate the importance of your words.

- *Do you brag on yourself?* People quit listening to those who are always talking about themselves. Learn to ask questions that show an interest in others. Leave it to other people to compliment you while you concentrate on the accomplishments of those around you.

- *Do you put others down, sometimes supposedly in fun?* The saying, "Many a truth is said in jest," is a truth in itself. Put-downs of any kind are never appropriate. Often, people degrade others in

19

an effort to lift themselves up, but just the opposite occurs. Degrading others makes you look bad.

- *Are you a negative person who always sees and tells the bad side of every situation?* Negative people pull others down with them, and people become weary of listening to criticism and negativity. Keep your pessimistic thoughts to yourself. Everyone needs to vent a little at times, but be careful that you are not concentrating on what is wrong, but rather on what is so often right.

- *Do you act conceited or give the impression that you know more than everyone else?* Conceit, an unrealistic opinion of yourself, is generally caused by low self-esteem and is highly unprofessional. Instead of giving the impression that you are better than everyone else, be yourself and learn to have confidence in your abilities.

- *Do you listen to the opinions of others?* People who think that they and they alone are always right can be very irritating. Be the kind of person who feels others have as much right to their opinions as you do to yours. You can both be right . . . or wrong.

- *Are you able to "read" the body language and nonverbal communication of others when you are speaking with them?* If the person with whom you are speaking is acting uninterested or bored, it may be time to stop talking or change the subject. People will generally let you know nonverbally if you are talking for too long or if you are saying things that are offensive.

- *Do you think you have to top the stories of others?* If someone is sharing something that happened to him, don't jump in to tell about something bigger and better that happened to you. Surely you know the kind of person who says things like, "Oh, that's nothing. I go to school full time, work four jobs to pay my tuition, and I've had pneumonia all semester!"

- *Are you careful not to interrupt other people when they are talking?* Really listen. Don't be thinking about what you are going to say next. Some people define listening as waiting until their turn

20

to speak. It is the height of rudeness to think that what you have to say is more important than what anyone else has to say.

- *Do you recognize what is currently considered to be "politically correct"?* Using a term that is now considered rude can be an embarrassing social blunder. For example, the term "Indian giver" has negative connotations for Native Americans.

- *Do you think before you speak, and are you aware of appropriate topics to discuss around others?* Watch what you talk about. Some topics are better left alone. Be aware of your audience and their interests and beliefs. Sensitivity and integrity should guide your conversations. Professionals don't ask personal or inappropriate questions such as, "How much money do you make?"

- *Do you ask permission if you use others' ideas?* If you notice another student or teacher using an idea you really like, ask permission before you use the idea and then give credit for its success. Most ideas are not original, and teachers are known for sharing their successes, but it is presumptuous to take someone's idea without permission or without giving proper credit.

- *Do you ever borrow money from colleagues or friends?* It is best not to borrow money from friends, even for a soda, but if you must, pay the money back that day or the next.

- *Are you defensive?* Some people carry grudges or hurts and tend to react to situations defensively. For example, if you've been excessively criticized about having a messy room, you might get angry quickly if anyone mentions something about your room. A defensive attitude can cloud your perception. People who have a "chip on their shoulder" can offend others without even knowing it.

- *How loudly, or softly, do you talk?* Pay attention to the voice levels of those around you. If your voice can be heard above the other voices in a room, then you are probably talking too loudly. It is also a social irritation when someone speaks so softly people have to strain to hear. Both situations make people uncomfortable.

- *Are you careful not to talk about others behind their backs?* People catch on quickly to the types who spread rumors or talk negatively about others. You can't trust people like that because next time it might be you they are talking about.

- *Are you polite?* Do you say "please" and "thank you" and treat others with respect? Kindness is one of the most important social skills you can practice.

If you recognized any problem areas as you read this list, don't be disheartened or discouraged. Just choose one area you'd like to work on first. Then make it a point to concentrate on that one area. Pay attention to what you do. Notice how others react to you as you make changes in yourself. Social etiquette is not a gift. It is a learned skill—and one that gets better with practice.

PROFESSIONAL ATTIRE

"Unless you're an artist at a very unconventional college, dress conservatively and professionally, so that the world will little note nor long remember what you wore" (Toth, 1999).

The best ways to determine the appropriate attire at your school are to ask other teachers or the principal and to pay attention to what your colleagues wear. Most schools have either a written or unwritten dress code. For example, one school may allow teachers to wear jeans while another school in the same district won't. If your school is one that allows you to wear jeans, make certain they are relatively new jeans with no holes or worn places. Find out the dress code for your school and follow it.

Sometimes it doesn't matter so much what type of clothing you wear, but whether you look dirty, wrinkled or sloppy. Also, you should make sure that what you are wearing is considered appropriate for a teacher. A teacher should look like the teacher, not one of the students. School is not the place to try to make wild fashion statements or to dress in provocative ways. For example, it is not appropriate for women to show cleavage or to wear extremely short dresses. Whatever the current style, you should be careful that underclothing does not show

22

when you are working with students.

Trends, such as low-riding jeans, body piercing, and tattoos, may be fine, but they are not the look of a professional at work. Just as your doctor dresses professionally, so should you. As a professional you should always be neat and clean and look your best. As principal Les Ford says, "Sometimes the key to being a professional is to look and act the part."

ATTENDANCE

"When the teacher is absent from the classroom, the students lose out."

—Janice Hogan, Principal

Attendance and punctuality are of the utmost importance for teachers. You will be allowed a certain number of sick days that are intended to be used strictly for that purpose. You should not use a sick day to attend a special function or take a trip. You are expected to be at school. Most schools, however, also provide personal and professional days. The personal days are intended for needs such as personal business, while professional days may be used to attend professional development workshops or conferences.

When you are asked to be at school for any reason whether it is for a PTA or PTO meeting, faculty meeting, workshop, or a dance, then you need to be there, and be there on time. Your administrator will let you know which activities are mandatory and which are optional. If it is unclear, ask.

You are expected to be at school on time, every time. Excuses like "I got stuck in traffic" don't count. It is your responsibility to be in your classroom when you are supposed to be there. In teaching, there is no one to "cover for you." Other teachers are busy in their own classrooms with their own students. If you expect them to assume responsibility for you because of your own lack of professionalism, you will quickly lose your colleagues' respect. When you have earned the reputation for good attendance and punctuality, and something unforeseen does occur, as it certainly will, your co-workers will not hesitate to help you.

DEVELOPING CONFIDENCE

"Confidence is attractive. Confidence puts people at ease."
—Lori Spiegel, Parent

*B*elieve it or not, some of the most common social errors come from a lack of confidence, which stems from a person's feelings of inferiority. It is sometimes difficult to have confidence as a beginning teacher. Everything seems unknown. You may feel knowledgeable in your subject area, but you worry about things such as getting your students' attention or motivating them. Once you experience some success in your classroom, the confidence will come. You'll feel pride when you do something right, and you'll learn to try again when you have a disaster. You'll get to know your students, and they'll get to know you, and you will grow comfortable with each other. As you develop and maintain a classroom atmosphere of mutual trust and respect (even when you don't like what your students are doing and they claim not to like you), your confidence as a teacher will grow. It will become stronger with each encounter with parents, administrators, and colleagues.

People who know their worth do not need to brag, won't have the need to top other people's stories, or be as apt to have a defensive nature. It's nice to be around people who are self-confident because they are not trying to impress you or put you down. They are not afraid to be themselves. They put you at ease. Because they are comfortable with themselves, they make you feel comfortable too.

Working on your self-confidence is often difficult because we believe the saying, "Don't tell him that; he'll get the big head." We've experienced the discomfort of being around people who are conceited. But conceit and confidence is not the same thing. According to Webster's, *conceit* is "an exaggerated opinion of oneself." Confidence is "belief in one's own abilities." It is good and healthy to know who you are and what you are capable of doing. Some feel that the most admirable trait a person can have is confidence in themselves. People who have self-confidence stand a little straighter, speak a little more clearly, and are almost impossible to offend. Most offenses come when we feel attacked in an area of weakness that we are trying to hide. If you can accept yourself just the way you are, then you won't need to cover up who you are.

As with social skills, confidence is something you can develop. It may seem there are more people with inferiority complexes than there are people with confidence. Yet, most have a strong desire to feel more confident. If you are one of those people, the following is a list of some things you might consider to help you realize your worth.

- *Frame your diploma.* Frame any awards you have received. Getting a college education is no small feat. You have to be *smart* to have passed all the tests; you have be *dedicated* to keep on going even on the days when you wanted to quit; you have to be *disciplined* to keep a schedule of everything you had to accomplish. You stayed the course; and you are most likely *happy* because you have reached or will soon reach the goal you have worked so hard to achieve. Revel in it.

- *"Nothing succeeds like success."* The more you succeed, the more confident you feel and become. As suggested above, a degree is a confidence builder. Think of other successes you have experienced and recognize that you are capable and competent. Set short-term and long-term achievable goals for yourself. As you reach them, stop and take note of your accomplishments.

- *Make a list of recent accomplishments.* Have you aced a test lately? Did you finally get something organized, such as your papers from last semester? Have you achieved a short-term goal such as saving money for that longed-for vacation? Seeing your accomplishments on paper might help you see that you've done more than you have.

- *Make a list of things that make you proud of yourself.* What do you like about yourself? Which of your traits do you most admire? What do others often compliment you on? Recognize your positive characteristics and celebrate them.

25

- *Concentrate more on evaluating yourself than on others' evaluations of you.* Don't let others' opinions of you negatively affect who you are. Be open to constructive criticism, but if after contemplation, you find it not fitting, let go of it. If you struggle in this area, take to heart the saying, "What you think of me is none of my business."

- *Work at trusting yourself and your instincts.* Take risks. Remember that it's okay to make mistakes because that's part of being human. As you practice trusting yourself, you will begin to see that you are capable and knowledgeable. The more you risk, the more you will succeed.

PART TWO

COMMUNICATING EFFECTIVELY

"The teacher uses knowledge of effective verbal, nonverbal, and media communication techniques to foster active inquiry, collaboration, and supportive interaction in the classroom" (Interstate New Teacher Assessment and Support Consortium Standards, 2004).

As a teacher, you are a communicator. Communicating is your business, and learning effective ways to express yourself will aid you not only in doing your job well, but also in getting along with people. Does what you say have substance? Is it beneficial? Analyze the words you use and the content of what you say and determine what kind of communicator you are.

How you speak is as important as what you say. Much can be inferred by listening to your tone of voice. An animal may not be able to understand many words, but it can get a clear picture of what is meant by its master's tone of voice. A teacher must pay careful attention to his or her tone when speaking with students. A severe tone can weaken even the most complimentary of words.

The written word is another area of communication used regularly by teachers. You must take care to communicate effectively on paper. Writing is simply "talk written down," so as you attempt to express yourself on paper to your students, parents, or administrators, be careful with the words you use, the standards of written language, and the proofing of your work.

STANDARD ENGLISH USAGE

"As a high school English teacher, even I had some grammar issues. When I began teaching an intense semester-long grammar class, I certainly learned some unfamiliar rules. Now, I try to use proper English as often as possible because hearing it helps students learn to master the language naturally."

—Kerri Cox, Teacher

*F*ar too often, teachers spend years preparing themselves for a teaching position, yet neglect one of the most noticeable areas of education—standard English. First impressions are very important, especially when working as a professional. In letters of application, in the interview process, and in classroom teaching itself, grammatical errors are indicators of carelessness. Though you may live in an area where it "sounds right" to use certain words or phrases, recognizing the difference between colloquialisms and standard English will cause you to stand above others professionally. Educating yourself as to the proper use of the English language is imperative if you want to be a successful role model to your students and present yourself in a professional manner to those with whom you come in contact. Some commonly misused words are illustrated in the following list. Again, evaluate yourself. If you find some areas of weakness, be deliberate about strengthening those areas. There is nothing magical about learning to speak properly. It takes time and effort—and the desire.

- Use "himself" rather than "hisself."

- Use "burst" rather than "bust."

- Use "especially" rather than "exspecially."

- Use "idea" rather than "ideal."

- Use "across" rather than "acrost."

- Use "could have" or "might have" rather than "could of" or "might of."

- Use "between" when referring to two; use "among" when referring to more than two.

- "Your" is possessive as in *your house*. "You're" is a contraction, as in *You're nice*.

- "Too" means too much or also, and is often confused with "to."

28

- Use "there" as in *There she is*. "Their" is a possessive pronoun, as in *It is their dog*. "They're" is a contraction—*They're my friends*.

- "Who's" is a contraction for "who is," as in *Who's at the door?* "Whose" is a possessive pronoun, as in *Whose house is that?*

- "Real" is an adjective, as in *That is a real problem*. "Very" is an adverb, as in *She is very nice*.

- "It's" is a contraction for "it is," as in *It's a nice day*. "Its" is a possessive pronoun, as in *The dog lost its collar*.

- "Sit" means to rest, as in *Today I sit down, yesterday I sat down, and I have sat down*. "Set" means "to place" and has an object, as in *Today I set the table, yesterday I set the table, and I have set the table*.

- "Lie" means to recline, as in *Today I lie down, yesterday I lay down, and I have lain down*. "Lay" means "to place" and has an object as in *Today I lay the book on the table, yesterday I laid the book on the table, and I have laid the book on the table*.

- "Affect" is a verb (remember **a** for action), as in *How did the storm affect you?* "Effect" is a noun, as in *What was the effect of the storm?*

- "Accept" means to receive, as in *Will you accept the gift?* "Except" means "all but," as in *Everyone except Bob went to the party*.

- "A lot" is always written as two words (never "alot").

- "All ready" means all are ready. "Already" means previously, as in *We have already eaten*.

- Use "does" or "doesn't" with a singular subject, as in *He doesn't work here*. Use "do" or "don't" with a plural subject or "you" or "I," as in *They don't work here*.

- "Saw" is the past tense of "see," as in *I saw you yesterday.* "Seen" is the past participle of "see" and needs a helping verb, as in *I have seen you twice this week.*

- "Went" is the past tense of "go," as in *I went to the store.* "Gone" is the past participle of "go" and needs a helping verb, as in *I have gone to the store.*

- "Good" is an adjective, as in *That was a good program.* "Well" is an adverb, as in *She sang well.*

- "Hardly" and "scarcely" are both negatives and should not be used with other negatives. Example: *I can hardly wait* (Not *I can't hardly wait*).

- Don't use "kind of" or "sort of" in formal writing; use "rather" or "somewhat" instead.

- "Them" is not used as an adjective; say *those boys* rather than *them boys.*

- Use "way" rather than "ways" when referring to distance, as in *They had a long way to go.*

- Use the pronoun "who" with people only; use "which" to refer to things only; use "that" to refer to either people or things.

- "Who's" is a contraction for who is, as in *Who's at the door?* "Whose" is a possessive pronoun, as in *Whose house is that?*

NONVERBAL COMMUNICATION

"In a college course on classroom discipline, I learned the importance of being able to give THE LOOK—you know, the one that firmly expresses disapproval without the need to use any words. As a 22-year-old first-year teacher, the art of the LOOK was beyond me, but after six years of teaching and two years of motherhood, I think I am finally quite able to give the LOOK when needed."

—Kerri Cox, Teacher

We can speak volumes without uttering a word. In his book, *Introduction to Sociology*, John Jay Bonstingle writes, "Sociologists say that over 90% of our communication is nonverbal." Tone of voice, eye contact, body language—all of these communicate. One's body language, a type of nonverbal communication in which body movements give messages, sometimes unconsciously can pull people into a conversation or push them away. Without saying a word, one can either acknowledge a person warmly or give him the cold shoulder. Both students and their parents may draw conclusions based on the body language of teachers. A professional must be aware of the messages he or she gives in the form of nonverbal communication as well as with words. Ritts and Stein (2004) contend, "It is not only what you say in the classroom that is important, but it's how you say it that can make the difference to students. Nonverbal messages are an essential component of communication in the teaching process."

Many teachers have learned that nonverbal communication can be used to keep discipline in the classroom. Teacher Russell Cox states, "When I began teaching, I thought every discipline problem required a verbal response, but as I gained more experience, I realized the best response is often dead silence. I think this works because the student already knows what he or she did, and it is hard to argue with silence."

Listening Skills

"When we assume the role of an active listener, we're communicating to whoever is speaking that we've heard them correctly and understood what they've said" (The Whole Child, 2004).

The speaker is not the only participant in a conversation. The listener plays an active role in any discussion. Have you ever tried to talk with someone who continually looked at his watch or looked at what was going on behind you? It is unnerving at best and unproductive at worst. When you find yourself in the listener role, concentrate on what the speaker is saying. Listen with your eyes as well as your ears. Acknowledge that you are hearing what is being said, either through words or a nod. It may even be appropriate to repeat back to the speaker what you thought you heard him say: "What I am hearing from you is... ."

Our classrooms often become places where teachers talk and students listen, and that's appropriate some of the time. But a classroom where students are talking and asking questions is a classroom where you can observe learning going on. Find every occasion you can to listen and respond to your students.

It has been said that we were given one mouth and two ears for a reason. There will be many times in your teaching profession when the best and most important thing you can do will be to listen; listen to students; listen to administrators; listen to peers; listen to parents. You might even find it necessary to listen to your heart.

TELEPHONE ETIQUETTE

"The telephone, so frequently seen as a personal communications tool in any school, has suffered the most from rude uses" (Lindsay, 1999, p. 34).

Telephone manners can help you get that coveted job interview. You will soon be calling schools asking for applications, job openings, and requests for interviews. Some administrators try to get a picture of you during a phone call before they actually invite you for an interview. Your telephone manners can be indicative of your overall social skills. Administrators are looking for people with professional qualities.

The following sentence should be more than obvious, but unfortunately, some people disregard its importance. When you are on a job interview, when you are teaching, or when you are speaking with a parent or administrator, turn off your cell phone. A true professional does not interrupt a meeting with someone to answer a cell phone. It is rude.

Telephones with voice mail are now common in many classrooms. If this is your situation, make your voice mail recording professional by leaving a brief message using a positive tone of voice, stating your name, the grade you teach or your subject area, and directions for how to best leave a message. Then be certain to check your messages daily and to return calls promptly—that day if possible.

Telephone Tips

- When you receive a telephone message, return the call as soon as you possibly can. Not returning calls, or returning them late, is very unprofessional. Never assume that "they'll call back if it's really important."

- Follow the 9-to-9 rule: Don't call people before 9:00 in the morning or after 9:00 at night.

- When you call someone, identify yourself immediately—even before asking for the person to whom you would like to speak. If people must guess to whom they are talking, it puts others on the spot and is unprofessional. This is especially true when calling the parents of your students. It would be most appropriate to say something like, "Hello. This is Mrs. Smith. I am Mark's English teacher." Then you may explain why you are calling. An exception to this rule would be when you call your mother.

- After identifying yourself, it is also polite to say something along the lines of, "Am I catching you at a bad time?" or "Do you have a moment to talk?"

- If someone calls you and does not identify himself, you may politely say, "May I ask who is calling?" It is unprofessional of the caller to force you to ask that question.

- When leaving a message on voice mail or on an answering machine, be sure to slowly and clearly state your name, phone number, the date and time, and the nature of your call. Keep your message short and to the point.

- If someone calls your house and asks to speak to you by name, reply, "This is she," or "This is he."

- Don't keep the other person on the phone longer than is necessary.

- A word about call-waiting. While many people have the service, it is still in bad taste to put people on hold—especially when you have called them. Unless you are expecting a call from the President of the United States or your wife who is 9 1/2 months pregnant, don't put people on hold.

WRITTEN COMMUNICATION

"All teachers, whether they realize it or not, are teachers of communication skills every time they speak or write."
-Candace Fisk, Teacher

Most parents like to know what is going on with their children at school whether those children are six or sixteen. Teachers know that and agree that home/school communication is vital. The problem with written communication is not that teachers aren't aware of the importance of keeping parents informed; the problem is making the time to do so. The problem is always time. When is a teacher supposed to write these necessary documents? Students will probably agree that there are too many hours spent in school, but when you become a teacher, you will discover that there just aren't enough hours in the school day.

Here is a thought: If teachers don't have enough time, and students have too much time, then perhaps teachers are working harder than their students. It has been said, "The person who is doing most of the work in the classroom is the person who is doing most of the learning" (Hurst, 1998, p. 23). If it's true that the person working is the person learning, then doesn't it follow that teachers are doing most of the learning? One way you can be sure that your students are working harder than you are, and thus learning, is to give some of your tasks to them. Look at each job you have and ask yourself: *Is this something my students could be doing?* For example, students from elementary school to high school would enjoy having a turn at producing the class newsletter—and they would learn so much in the process.

Some forms of written communication will out of necessity have to come directly from the teacher. It will be a necessary part of your planning to include them. From introductory letters to grade checks, from school calendars to field trips, permission slips, and little notes of praise—whatever the forum, the more you communicate with parents, the better off everyone will be.

Newsletters

"I send a newsletter to parents before I ever meet my students. I introduce myself with a short personal and professional biography. I include sayings, poems, pictures, and an invitation for both students and parents to become active members of our class."

—Gina Cowin, Teacher

One of the most efficient ways to keep your parents informed is through weekly, monthly, or quarterly newsletters. Using a computer, your newsletter can be set up at the beginning of the year and then adapted each time you publish it. Many word processing programs come with templates for newsletters, which make them quick and easy to create. A variety of topics can be included in your class newsletter. (See Appendix G for a sample newsletter.) Below is a list of items you might consider.

- List of objectives that were covered that week and/or a list of objectives that will be covered next week.

- Assignments for the week.

- List of the week's spelling words.

- Information about upcoming activities.

- Student of the week.

- Classroom accomplishments.

- Samples of student work.

- Class activities.

- Extracurricular activities (PTA meetings, music concerts).

Importance of Proofreading

"No matter how confident you are of your writing skills, you should always have a second set of eyes look over any document you are sending out. Sometimes the writer overlooks the silliest typos. People have high expectations of teachers, so you want your documents to be perfect."

—Russell and Kerri Cox, Teachers

Sending home correspondence that contains mistakes is one of the most unprofessional things you can do as a teacher. Of all people, teachers should know the importance of error-free correspondence. When parents receive a note from their child's teacher with a mistake, it causes a lack of confidence in the teacher and concern about their child's education.

In the process of writing, the step of revision is very different from the step of proofreading. As you write items for parents, students, or administrators, spend a little extra time with the writing process. When you revise what you have written, you are re-reading it with a critical eye. You might ask yourself, "Have I said what I intended to say? Are the points I want to make in the best order for reader understanding? Are there sentences that are irrelevant? Have I been too wordy?" Answering these questions will help you create a finished product that makes sense to the reader, is clear, and shows your professionalism.

When you proofread what you have written, you are looking for specific grammatical, mechanical, or structural errors. Read and reread your product. Teachers have many responsibilities and often hurry with paperwork, and it is easy to overlook minor (and sometimes not so minor) errors in something they have written. Not only is a poorly written or inadequately proofed letter sent home to parents unprofessional, but it defies what you are trying to teach your students: to put their best foot forward, to take the time to make the extra effort, and to take pride in their work. If you are weak in writing skills or don't feel secure in catching mistakes, have someone you trust proof your writing for you. The following list will remind you of common errors in writing.

- *Capitalization.* You should capitalize all proper nouns and the beginning letter of every sentence (unless it is a sentence that comes after a semicolon). You should not capitalize seasons of the year or school subjects that are not languages or that do not have a Roman numeral after them (For example, *English, science, social studies, Algebra II)*. Do not capitalize directions unless they are used as a region of the country, as in *I traveled **west** on State Street,* and *I learned that the **North** had won the Civil War.*

- *Punctuation.* Be sure that all sentences have the proper end punctuation. Do not use commas to connect two sentences unless you are also using a conjunction (and, or, but, etc.). Do not overuse commas; there should be a reason for every comma used. A reference book that highlights punctuation rules will give you specifics for the many types and uses of punctuation.

- *Grammar.* As discussed previously in the communication section, usage is very important. The same rules apply in writing as in speaking. It is advisable to use a reference book for any questions you may have as to the correct usage of a word.

- *Run-on sentences.* The comma splice is one of the most common errors in written communication. This occurs when two complete sentences are connected with a comma, as in *We will have conferences on March 17, they will last all day.* Never use a comma to separate two complete sentences unless you also use a conjunction—*We will have conferences on March 17, and they will last all day.* Another common mistake people make in their writing is to run two complete sentences together with no punctuation, as in *I got to meet Marco's family they were very nice.* Be sure to include end punctuation at a sentence's end.

- *Sentence Fragments.* A complete sentence must have a subject, a verb, and be a complete thought. Far too often, people use inappropriate fragments in their writing. *Since I was going to work on my master's degree* is not a complete sentence. It cannot stand by itself as an independent thought. To correct the sentence, either remove *"Since"* or finish the thought—*Since I was going to work on my master's degree, I knew that my time for entertainment would be limited.* Fragments are easy to catch in your writing if you proof carefully.

Spelling Errors

There is no reason to send anything in writing with a misspelled word, especially with today's technology. Computers have a spell check function, dictionaries are readily available, and electronic spellers abound. Any time you are in doubt about the spelling of a word, look it up or ask. There is nothing wrong with asking someone how to spell a word. There is quite a lot wrong with taking a guess at it, especially if your written product is for others.

It is always a good idea, especially if spelling does not come naturally to you, to have someone proofread your work. This simply shows conscientiousness on your part. Do not implicitly trust the spell check function on a computer; the computer does not have a brain. It does not know whether you want to spell "there" or "their." Even the grammar checks are not foolproof. Don't trust a machine to do your thinking for you. Letters of application with misspelled words give a negative impression. It is quite possible that it will get no further, for improper spelling shows a lack of diligence on the part of the writer.

Email

"The integration of email in the K-12 classroom has much potential, and technology-confident teachers must become products of education" (Blake, Holcombe, & Foster, 1998, p. 49).

Email, or electronic mail, has become a fast and easy method of correspondence. As technology continues to advance in personal home usage, many parents appreciate being able to contact their children's teachers via email. It is convenient for correspondence between teachers and parents and can eliminate the problem of playing "telephone tag." Email is also an easy way for teachers to send weekly class letters to parents to keep them informed about classroom activities and news. Many school districts provide their teachers with email accounts and expect them to check their mail for important announcements and correspondence. Check your mail regularly and respond promptly.

Some people think that the rules of writing such as capitalization and punctuation do not apply to email. That may be true if you are emailing your best friend from high school, but a professional email message needs to be as carefully written as a typed business letter. Reread your message after you've written it, using the same editing and rewriting techniques you would normally use. And, of course, you should always use the spell check function before sending your message. Email messages should be short and to the point.

A word of caution about email messages: The writer's tone is not always discernable, so choose your words carefully. Email messages can also be forwarded on to others; don't say anything in an email message you may later regret.

PART THREE

BUILDING RELATIONSHIPS

"A professional is one who has the ability to treat co-workers and students with respect in spite of our personal differences or opinions."
—Joyce Crumpley, Teacher

As a teacher, you will come in contact with hundreds of people each year. You will be building new relationships with teachers, students, parents, administrators, and the public. Some of these people will be acquaintances, some will be colleagues, and some will become very dear friends. The way you choose to handle yourself in these many relationships will make a difference in the success you have in the teaching profession. Building good, strong relationships is part of being a professional.

TEACHER TO TEACHER

"A professional teacher works cooperatively with other colleagues to best meet the needs of the students."
—Deana Glasgow, Teacher

When you get your first teaching job, don't take lightly the task of building relationships with the teachers in your building. Do as children are taught to do at a crosswalk: *Stop, look, and listen.* Notice which teachers seem to enjoy being teachers. Hang around those who laugh often, who can see the lighter sides of situations, and who make you feel good just being around them. Think about the kind of teacher you most want to be. If you want to be happy and enthused about being a teacher, then associate with people who are like that.

Working in a school is like working in a community. You will encounter people you admire and respect and you will find people who are difficult and perhaps even obnoxious. Making the decision to develop good working relationships with the people with whom you work will be one of your first tests of professionalism. You are not competing with your peers; you are working with them as a team. You must be secure enough to recognize their strengths and their weaknesses as just those—strengths and weaknesses. You cannot wear your feelings on your sleeve and live in turmoil over every little thing that bothers you. Likewise, you cannot stay awake nights wondering why you can't do such and such as well as so and so.

Managing School Politics Effectively

"When the school politics get rough, as they often do, I go back to the origin of my mission—to make a difference in the lives of kids, thereby helping to make the world a better place for all of us" (Hurst & Reding, 1999, p. 11).

—Justine Lines, Teacher

*A*ny time you deal with people, there will be personality conflicts. Situations won't always be fair, and people will always talk. These are the kinds of things that can dampen your spirits if you're not careful. A certain amount of involvement in the "office politics" is unavoidable, but how immersed you become is up to you. As the saying goes, "Choose your battles carefully." For example, if there is a problem with the new faculty insurance plan, you may want to get involved and try to offer solutions to work it out. If your school has a salary schedule that has been improved, but not to your satisfaction, you will need to choose whether you will invest your time fretting over it and complaining about it or accepting it until the next opportunity for your input. When it comes to dealing with school politics, the most professional approach you can take is to closely adhere to the rules of social etiquette.

One of those most important rules of social etiquette is one you have heard all your lives: don't gossip or speak unkindly or inappropriately to or about others. Teaching this concept and practicing it in your own school workroom are two different things. An old story is told of a woman who was notorious for spreading gossip. When she realized one day the negative impact she was having on those around her, she went to her clergyman to ask how she could take back all of the things she had said about others. Carrying a feather pillow, he took her up to the bell tower of the church. He ripped the pillow open and let the feathers fall into the wind. He then told her that when she had collected all of the feathers from the pillow to come back and he would tell her the answer she was seeking. She objected, saying there was no way she could find every feather from the pillow. "And neither can you take back all of the words you have spoken," he said. Once words of gossip are spoken, they spread like the feathers in the wind and are impossible to gather back in. Be careful what you say. Be careful what you listen to. Even listening to negative talk can bring you down.

The best way to keep school politics in perspective is to remember why you became a teacher in the first place. Keep your focus on your students and temper decisions about what's important by what is best for them.

Being a Team Player

Teachers "are team players willing to share their knowledge and skill with others and participate in the ongoing development of strong school programs" (National Board for Professional Teaching Standards, 2004).

Professionals work together. They understand the concept that "It takes a whole village to raise a child." Work with other teachers, parents, and administrators to meet the needs of your students. If you have a student who has an Individual Education Plan (IEP), work closely with members of that child's educational team. Ask questions. Find out ways you can help.

School boards and administrators will often want their teachers' involvement in creating school visions or new types of programs. Recognize that your input is valuable and needed. When you serve on committees or are asked to work with other teachers to develop a new program or choose new textbooks, strive to work together to meet your goals. Be a willing participant and do your part.

It is disruptive to a faculty, and in the end to the children being served, if a teacher consistently refuses to work as a team member. Though there is something admirable about those who "follow their own drummer," there is a time when that attitude is appropriate and a time when it is not. For the good of the students and the school, sometimes you must compromise your own ideas or plans and cooperate with others.

Supporting Your Colleagues

"Teachers need to support each other as much as possible to encourage positive attitudes within the school and community" (Hurst & Reding, 1999, p. 123).

—Monica Andrews, Teacher

*S*howing support to your colleagues is a significant part of being a professional. Be quick to encourage the teachers with whom you work. When you see someone in need of a kind word or a helping hand, offer your assistance. Being a new teacher in a new school can be very lonely. Be deliberate about reaching out and making yourself available. Teachers may form cliques, knowingly or unknowingly, which jeopardize relationships between the faculty members as a whole. Guard against being a part of a group that might tear down rather than build up.

Even though you work with many teachers, there will be times when you may feel alone and isolated in your own classroom. Remember that others are feeling the same way. It takes effort, but effort that will be rewarded in kind, to go out of your way to support and encourage your colleagues.

TEACHER TO STUDENT

"Being a teacher is not about being up on a pedestal and simply disseminating information to the students—it's a reciprocal adventure whereby each day we teachers present the opportunity for students to learn and grow, and they, in turn, do the same for us."

—Christine Santhuff, Teacher

A baby food company used to have an advertising slogan that said, "Babies are our business, our only business." Likewise, teachers can say of their work: "Students are our business, our only business." It is true that on a teacher workday when no students are present, things may go very smoothly and much planning and work will get accomplished. However, too many days without students defeats the purpose of the preparation; as a teacher, you cannot do your job without students because your students are your business.

It is of utmost importance to develop a good working relationship with your students. They need to be able to understand you; they need to trust you; they need to be able to talk with you. Being friends with your students should not be a priority; they need the security of knowing that you are more than a friend, that you have their best interest at heart, and that you are determined to carry out the purpose for which you are there.

Students Are Your Focus

"Every child has at least one redeeming quality; as teachers, it is our job to find it and build on it."

—Nelwyn Mathews, Teacher

As a teacher, you will find that a variety of things will compete for your attention. Meetings, paperwork, committee responsibilities, conferences; any number of obligations may fill your calendar. Being a professional means knowing your mission; it means remembering your focus. The reason you are in the classroom is to benefit the student. As an educator, you are a facilitator to learning; your students should always be uppermost in your mind as you plan your lessons and strive to accomplish your goals. There will be times when you will have to make choices, and often these decisions will not be easy to make. However, if you find yourself involved in too many things, even good things, you will soon realize that you are "robbing Peter to pay Paul." In other words, something is being shortchanged, and it certainly should not be your students. If you are not able to focus on their needs because of other distractions of your job, reevaluate your commitments. You must continually remind yourself of your purpose in teaching.

Teachers as Role Models

"Teaching is a public activity; a teacher works daily in the gaze of his or her students, and the extended nature of their lives together in schools places special obligations on the teacher's behavior" (National Board for Professional Teaching Standards, 2004).

Whether you like it or not, the nature of your job as a teacher makes you a role model to your students. There are teachers who excel in this role, encouraging by their own actions responsibility, love for learning, and the advantages of being a productive contributor to society. Unfortunately, the opposite is also true. The media has

44

provided the public with ample examples of teachers who have been poor role models—those who have become sexually involved with their students, or teachers who participate in illegal drug activity or have a criminal history. A poor role model, however, is not limited to a person who has done something illegal. A teacher who is not honest, who is not consistent, who is not fair, or who displays selfishness models in a negative way.

What kinds of things can you do to provide a good example for your students? Show your concern for them and for society as a whole; be on guard as to how you respond to your circumstances; share with them your love for learning—they will catch it; talk with them about what you read, making sure that you often read things on their level; be consistent, practicing what you preach. Teachers who practice self-discipline and make a conscious choice to contribute something positive to those with whom they come in contact will impact those lives far beyond their own knowledge. You may not always feel like listening, following through with a promise made, or trying to explain something just one more time. But through self-discipline you can say, "I will do it even though I may not feel like it," and that is what will make the difference.

Student Conferences

"A teacher's foremost responsibility is to the intellectual development of our youth, but they are mindful of the broad range of children's needs, including the need for guidance and the strong presence of caring and nurturing adults" (National Board for Professional Teaching Standards, 2004).

One of the most rewarding parts of teaching is working one on one with individual students. Conferencing with them provides an

effective means of doing so. Nearly any age group can benefit from student conferences, and the teacher can adapt the conference to any age.

A student conference consists of a period of time when the teacher and student meet together to discuss a particular topic. Student conferences may be used for disciplinary issues, academics, goal setting, and so on.

Ideally, conferences are short, to the point, and regularly held.

One example of an effective student conference is used in the reading workshop. The teacher meets with each student for a brief period of time. During this time, the student may set goals for reading progress, report to the teacher what book is presently being read, discuss the book being read, and ask or answer questions about the book. Both teacher and student share, and they both listen. Remember that this is a brief conference. The goal is to be able to meet with each student; if too much time is given to some, others will be neglected.

Student conferencing not only helps the student academically, but it gives an opportunity for communication between student and teacher. The more positive contacts a teacher can make with the student, the better off both of them are. Conferences give teachers an opportunity to recognize problems the student may be having and also increase the probability of positive feedback. It is important to briefly interact with each student individually at least one time during the day. This may not sound like too difficult a task, but it is surprising how often the same students are involved in teacher/student interaction and others are left out.

Earning Respect

"Professionalism involves not only what you say and do, but also what you allow or don't allow to be said or done in your classroom."
—Janice Hogan, Principal

Certain positions demand respect simply because of the nature of the position. A teacher, however, cannot expect to be respected simply because he or she is "the teacher." That day is past. A teacher earns the

respect of his or her students and their parents by acting in a professional manner and treating others appropriately.

Too often, a teacher who is demanding, harsh, or critical with students in the classroom will become upset when their responses are not positive ones. Likewise, if a teacher teases a student, perhaps in a cruel way, the student may react in the same way; then the teacher may discipline the child for disrespectful conduct. This is, at best, very confusing to the students, and at worst, a recipe for disaster in the classroom.

Teachers must regard each student as a person of worth. Children should be treated with kindness and concern. This in no way means that teachers should not have high expectations for their students. It is important to be consistent and fair, and very often it is necessary to be firm. A child can easily recognize the difference between a teacher who cares and who values his or her students and one who does not. The teacher who respects his students will be one who will receive that same honor in return. Being respected does not mean being best friends. It may not even mean being liked. Teachers should not seek to win a popularity contest, but rather earn the respect of their students.

Being Fair

"As stewards for the interests of students, accomplished teachers are vigilant in ensuring that all pupils receive their fair share of attention, and that biases based on real or perceived ability differences, handicaps or disabilities, social or cultural background, language, race, religion, or gender do not distort relationships between themselves and their students" (National Board for Professional Teaching Standards, 2004).

As mentioned earlier, a fair teacher is an effective teacher. Students are quick to recognize justice and are demanding of it. Most will readily take their due punishment or face the consequences of a misdeed if they understand that the result is fair. Likewise, they expect their peers to be treated equally. If one student is treated in a noticeably different way than the others without a just cause, students will recognize the injustice and problems may arise. Children are merciful in many ways, especially in unusual circumstances. For example, students will often be understanding of a teacher who gives some slack to a student who is acting out if they are aware that the student is experiencing severe home problems.

It is interesting to note that children are often tougher on their own peers than are their adult instructors. They want an environment that is structured, one that they can count on being consistent, and one that is fair. They want boundaries set, and they want someone to enforce them. If peers determined consequences, justice would most often be swift and severe.

Teachers who act in a professional manner make certain that their classrooms operate fairly. They consider what they say and do before acting, and make the effort to look at things through their students' perspectives.

TEACHER TO PARENT

"Teachers share with parents the education of the young. They communicate regularly with parents and guardians, listening to their concerns and respecting their perspective, enlisting their support in fostering learning and good habits, informing them of their child's accomplishments and successes, and educating them about school programs" (National Board for Professional Teaching Standards, 2004).

The old proverb "An ounce of prevention is worth a pound of cure" applies to the relationship between teacher and parent. Establishing a good working alliance between the two is vital for a child's positive learning experience.

As a teacher, you will need to take the initiative in establishing a relationship with your students' parents. Often this will be a very easy thing to do, as most parents are eager to be involved in their children's education and will be in touch regularly with you. In other cases, it will be more difficult. You will need to be the one to make an effort to communicate consistently, be open about things that are going on in your classroom, and give parents the reassurance that you are readily available if they have questions or concerns.

Make an effort to get to know your students. If parents see that you know their children and have their best interest at heart, the parent/teacher relationship will be better. Making a positive contact with parents early in the year is a good idea. Then, if later you must talk about a problem, the parents have some background of a positive contact from you. Let parents know you are available and give them a way to contact you. You may do this through an open-house night, a class letter that goes out to each parent, letter to parents posted on your web page, an email message, a phone call, or a personal note.

When parents and teachers understand that they are on the same side and that both want the best for the child, problems can be solved more easily or even prevented from occurring. Teacher Yvonne Heath has found "Parents can be a teacher's greatest ally. Once you are in the same court, you can accomplish great things for the good of the students."

Communication Is Key

"Teachers must have a deep knowledge and skill base to serve students with a wide range of learning and social needs and to be able communicate those needs to parents."
—Emmett Sawyer, Principal

*P*reventing problems with parents can be as easy as learning a few communication skills. As mentioned earlier, it is extremely important to have a positive first contact with parents. This can be done in a variety of ways. Some teachers of young students make summer visits to the homes of the children who will be enrolling in their classes in the fall. They may take with them a book or some other item of interest to present to the child when they introduce themselves to the future student and his or her family. Other teachers write letters to each student and parent before the year starts to introduce themselves and to express excitement about the coming year.

Another good idea is to phone parents early in the school year with a positive report, such as letting them know about something at which their child has excelled or just letting them know you are glad to have their child in your class. Making positive contacts early in the year gives the teacher an advantage if later it is necessary to report something that may not be so eagerly received.

While it might be difficult to make individual calls if you have too many students, newsletters, brief notes, grade checks, and a variety of other types of communication will help to establish a relationship

49

between teacher and parent. You can avoid confusion between home and school with good communication. The parent will remember a good conversation with a teacher who cares about the child and thus will be more likely to listen to what the teacher has to say.

Developing Partnerships

"A friendly, healthy relationship with parents will put everyone at ease and help the school year progress smoothly and successfully."
—Stephanie Hawn, Teacher

Working as a professional involves productive working relationships. Parent and teacher must have an understanding that the best interest of the child is the main issue in any situation. If the teacher recognizes that his or her student is also someone's child, it will be much easier for that teacher to understand parental responses.

Parents and teachers are on the same side and should strive to act accordingly. The teacher can model this idea of partnership in a variety of ways. Parents do not need to be at the school or in the classroom at all times, but they should be welcomed at any time. Give parents the opportunity to participate in their child's education. Ask for parental involvement with reading, working on projects, and responding to portfolios. Provide parents with opportunities to be a partner with the school.

Partnership is as much an attitude as anything else. Seeing parents as allies rather than the enemy is the beginning of positive working relationships with the adults in the lives of the children you teach.

Parent Conferences

"Treat each parent with dignity and respect; treat them like you want your child's teacher to treat you."

—Patsy Bowser, Teacher

One of the most frightening things to a beginning teacher is a face-to-face meeting with a student's parents. New teachers are often told horror stories of enraged parents with flared nostrils and lawsuits in hand, so it is no wonder that a parent conference is a dreaded event.

There are several keys to preparing for the conference between parent and teacher that will set the stage for smooth sailing.

- *Be prepared.* Before the conference, collect samples of the student's work, have your grade book or computer grade sheet handy, and gather any disciplinary records to which you may need to refer. It is a good idea to make notes ahead of time regarding any special comments you want to make.

- *Sandwich negative comments between positive ones.* As mentioned earlier, this student is someone's child. His or her parents may be as frustrated (or more so) as you are with particular problems, and they need to hear a kind word about their child. There is always something positive that can be pointed out about a person, and it is your job to find some of those things to convey to parents. When they hear that you recognize some of the good qualities of their child, they will be much more likely to accept the negative comments that you are obligated to share. It is also important that you provide some constructive suggestions for responding to the negative behaviors or poor skills that you are pointing out. Suggest specific ways parents can combat these problems at home.

- *Be pleasant.* People in general respond better to consideration and sensitivity than to harshness and severe criticism. You can be honest without being cruel.

- *Be prompt and stay on a time schedule,* especially if you have other parents waiting to conference with you at a particular time. Some parents will want to linger and continue to talk, which can destroy a schedule on a conference day or night. Stand, shake hands, and thank them for coming, reminding them that there is another parent scheduled for this time.

- *The teacher is in control of the meeting.* Take control of the situation early. Don't sit while parents stand looking down at you. Provide a comfortable place for them to sit, and then sit across from them where you can have good eye contact. Take the initiative to express your compliments and concerns about the student. Ask the parents if they have questions or areas of concern. Lead the discussion and make it a point to stay on topic. When the time for the conference is over, stand and lead the parents to the door.

Responding to Angry Parents

"In dealing with an unruly student or angry parent, if we respond in a hateful, sarcastic, or cutting manner, our success will be jeopardized."
—Janice Hogan, Principal

Sometimes new teachers think that if they are good enough teachers, they won't have problems with parents. Unfortunately, that's rarely the case. You might do a student activity, which 99% of the parents think was the product of a genius. But there will be that one parent who is disgruntled and wants to tell you about it. You will never be able to please everybody all of the time. You just have to do the best you can in your classroom and with your students each day. If a problem with a parent does arise, deal with it as professionally as possible. Keep your voice level and calm, find out what the concern is, and work toward a solution together.

If you have an angry parent approach you, you may feel attacked. You will probably feel hurt and perhaps even be angry yourself. What should your response be?

- *Ask your administrator, school counselor, or team teachers to meet with you if you are aware that you will be speaking with an angry parent.* Extra support is beneficial, and it often cools the parents' ire if they see that you are not the only teacher with whom they will be speaking or when they recognize that others in the school setting recognize similar problems with their child.

- *One of the most important things you can do is to listen.* Sometimes all a parent needs is a chance to vent. During the discussion, you may even discover that other things are going on in the person's life that are causing the frustration. Take time to listen before you get defensive and jump in with both feet.

- *Your reaction is very important.* It is not always how you act that speaks to others, but how you react. Stay calm as you respond. Responding positively is a difficult thing to do if you feel attacked. But it is important that you do just that. You may need to repeat back to the individual things that he or she is saying to you. This not only clarifies your understanding of what is being said, but also allows the parent the opportunity to hear how what he is saying is being heard. If you feel that there has been a misunderstanding, express your position to the parents in a calm, dignified manner. More often than not, angry parents just want to be heard and acknowledged, and an appropriate response by a teacher or administrator will calm the waters. A productive conference occurs when the parent sees that the teacher's main concern is the student's welfare.

- *Admit it when you make a mistake and take appropriate measures to correct it.* You will undoubtedly be wrong in some instances. Be big enough to recognize those times. Most people will respect those who are willing to admit their own errors. However, it is also important to be fair. Don't be bullied into something by one parent that will not apply to all of your other students. There is a line here that is important to draw.

- ***End the conference if nothing beneficial is occurring and you are being verbally abused.*** You do not have to listen to foul language or threats. There is nothing wrong with telling parents that you appreciate their viewpoint, steering them in the direction of the school office, buzzing in on the office intercom, or hanging up the phone if the anger is not controlled.

When a Parent Is Uninvolved

"I have had to understand that some of my students are coming from tough homes where parents don't always care, and the kids often lack basic skills you would think they should have. Teachers have to realize that with love and acceptance students will perform."

—Todd Varhalla, Teacher

Even an angry parent cares. It is hard to understand the apathetic or uninvolved parent, and even harder to know how to deal with him or her. Too many students get themselves up in the morning, face the day without the encouragement or support of a parent, and confront their problems on their own. Parents have been known to tell teachers that they have given up on their children or that they don't care what happens so long as the school keeps them (parents) out of it. In upper level classes, students may be living on their own without any parental involvement. Teachers often find that they are their students' support, and school becomes the safe place to be.

The truth is that some people are so caught up in their own lives that they don't make time for or spend the energy on their children. Whether this is a result of the parents being truly apathetic, or bound by their own struggles or vices, the results are much the same. Kids raise themselves. A strong teacher faces the reality of this and does not expect what will not be given.

What should you do with or for kids in this situation? You may become a liaison between the student and available resources. Depending upon the community, a variety of resources is available for kids who lack parental support. Boys' and Girls' Club programs are often available. Community members may have been trained to work with students. Big Brother and Big Sister programs are often offered.

If your school has a caseworker, he or she would be able to intercede and help you match that child with someone who cares. Many schools also offer after-school activities or programs for students.

You may find yourself the role model in this child's life. You can't take every child home with you to raise, but you can be a force of stability where you are. Your students should know that you are dependable, honest, and steady. They need you to be caring, but they also need for you to hold them accountable.

TEACHER TO ADMINISTRATOR

"When both administration and faculty place an unwavering focus on what constitutes learning in the children, then there is a constant source of renewable energy" (Graves, 2001, p. 154).

Authority plays an important role in our society. Everyone comes under someone else's authority. Even the person who owns his own business and is his own boss is not exempt from following certain codes, guidelines, and laws. In our society we give some people authority over various aspects of our lives such as where we park or how we drive. This concept is reinforced every time we receive a parking ticket. Sometimes we think if the sign says, "Don't park here," it magically doesn't apply to us. But the parking ticket still must be paid. In a school system, that authority is your administrator. The kind of respect you show your administrator is the same kind of respect your students should show for you.

It will be to your advantage, and to the advantage of the school itself and your students, if you learn to work with administrators rather than against them. What kind of relationship you have with them is largely up to you as a teacher. You should do all that you can to ensure a positive, productive relationship with those in authority.

Recognize the Role of the Administrator

"Looking at issues through our administrators' perspectives will help us better understand some of their decisions" (Hurst & Reding, 1999, p. 101).

Each school system has a chain of command to which teachers are responsible to adhere. Above the teacher's role in the chain are the principal, school superintendent, and school board. In larger school districts there may also be any number of department heads or curriculum directors.

It is important for teachers to recognize their role in this chain of command. A good administrator gets input from the staff, but once made, policies are to be followed. Although not everyone may be pleased with every decision, it is the teacher's responsibility to be supportive of that decision and to follow it.

Some teachers have difficulty recognizing the authority of those in positions above them. An aspect of being a professional is the ability to be a follower as well as a leader. Strong leadership qualities abound in the teaching profession. Good teachers must be strong leaders, but good teachers must also be willing to follow their administrators' leadership. This is not a sign of weakness, but a sign of discipline. It is definitely an indicator of one who is acting in a professional manner. It is the administrator's role to lead and guide, and a successful educator recognizes that.

Keep Your Administrator Informed

"I have found that administrators are generally eager to hear what we and our students are doing, and by telling them, we are offering them opportunities to celebrate with us" (Hurst & Reding, 1999, p. 101).
—Faye Sturhahn, Teacher

A principal needs to be made aware of certain situations or circumstances. In some cases it is better to over-inform than to under-inform. Administrators are put in precarious positions when a parent, community member, or school board member approaches them about an issue of which they are totally ignorant. It is to everyone's advantage to prevent this type of situation from occurring. The classroom teacher has the opportunity and responsibility to be a part of the solution to this problem.

If a teacher is consistently having trouble with a student or a parent, it is a good idea to discuss it with the principal. Administrators are busy people. They don't have time to discuss all the in's and out's of every situation, but a brief note or visit just to inform them of the situation is helpful. Concerns about curriculum decisions, faculty unrest, discipline issues, and academic weaknesses are all areas of interest to the administrator.

Building principals have an investment in the educational process that is occurring in their schools. Invite them into your classroom. Let them see first-hand what is going on. Welcome them into the learning environment you are creating, and keep them informed.

Follow Administrative Directives

"In any situation, you need to realize that your administrator has the best interest of the school, the staff (including you), and the students in mind. Do your best to follow the directives set before you."
—Stephanie Hawn, Teacher

When a directive is given, it is given for a reason. It is the teacher's responsibility to follow the administration's requests. Unless there is a question of morality or legality involved, a professional will cooperate with and support those in authority. There will of course be times when there is disagreement, and there will also be appropriate times to discuss these areas of contention. But when points have been made, discussion has been held, and the administrator's directive stands, the teacher's obligation is to comply.

It is not professional to ignore a policy, forcing the administrator to make an issue of it. For example, if a dress code for teachers directs them not to wear jeans to school, the teacher should comply with that request. Don't show up in jeans and wait to be told not to wear them again. Working as a team adds to the harmony of a school, and rebelling even in small ways against the desires of the administration tears down the school's unity.

Most schools have a committee or a liaison group that can address the concerns of the faculty to the principal. If a principal insists upon an action that faculty members strongly oppose, have a representative from the committee approach the principal to discuss the issue.

PART FOUR

PRACTICING PROFESSIONAL RESPONSIBILITIES

"Because they work in a field marked by many unsolved puzzles and an expanding research base, teachers have a professional obligation to be lifelong students of their craft, seeking to expand their repertoire, deepen their knowledge and skill, and become wiser in rendering judgments" (National Board for Professional Teaching Standards, 2004).

Much more than teaching is involved in being a professional. Teachers are expected to participate in activities outside their classrooms such as serving on committees and sponsoring clubs. Professionals are also expected to stay current with new research and up-to-date practices in their field. You wouldn't want to go to an accountant who doesn't know the latest tax laws, and you don't want to be a teacher who isn't aware of current research findings in your field. You can stay current by taking college courses and attending workshops and conferences provided by your school and other professional organizations.

SCHOOL RESPONSIBILITIES

One of the most frustrating parts of teaching is dealing with the responsibilities tied to the job that do not actually involve teaching. Sometimes teachers begin to feel that their teaching is suffering because of all the other things they are required to do. Some of these activities are necessary and beneficial, while others may be of questionable value to the educational process. Regardless, every teacher is expected to be involved in a number of activities other than the actual teaching process, and it is wise to be prepared for them.

Committee Work

"The effective committee member must be vocal but not verbose, humorous but not biting, serious but not funereal, conscientious but not compulsive, knowledgeable but not arrogant, prepared to defend

what he or she has said but not defensive, cooperative but not submissive, and civically responsible but not overly conformist" (Smelser, 1998, p. 35).

"A committee of one gets things done" is a popular saying. However, most committees are made up of more than one person, and many schools have so many committees that they have a committee for committees. Actually, the role of the committee is very important and is useful in keeping the school functioning well. Some examples of school committees are discipline, attendance, teacher welfare, and scholarship. In most schools, teachers are asked to volunteer to be on one or more committees so that they are working in an area of interest. A teacher has the responsibility to be actively involved as a part of this process and to attend all meetings. The more input the staff of a school has, the more cohesiveness and productivity there will be.

After School Functions and Extracurricular Activities

*E*ach school system has a variety of after-school activities that teachers are required to attend or sponsor. Most principals require their faculty members to be present at teachers' meetings throughout the school year. Some administrators plan their meetings on a regular basis, such as every week on a particular day, or monthly, such as on the first Wednesday of the month. Others call meetings as they are needed. As a professional, you must make it a point to attend these meetings. They provide needed information for teachers and present an opportunity for staff to interact and discuss issues. Meetings are held either before or after school and are not usually during actual contracted time. You will find that many of the things you are responsible for will be done on your own time.

Another after-school responsibility is the sponsorship of classes, clubs, or organizations such as Future Teachers of America. Leading an extracurricular activity can be an overwhelming responsibility, especially in regard to the amount of time spent. More often on the high school level, but at times also on the middle school and elementary levels, teachers are assigned classes to sponsor (freshman, sophomore, junior, senior). A sponsor may be asked to participate in fund raisers, chaperone dances, or work concession stands. Students are encouraged to be active in clubs, which produces a need for faculty sponsors. Clubs such as Future Business Leaders of America, Student Council, Technology Club, Drama Club, and other academic clubs all require adult leadership. Sponsorships take time, energy, and organization. While challenging, they can also be rewarding, especially if you find those that fit your interests.

Teachers are often asked to tutor students with special needs, to work the gate at ball games, to participate in incentive plans for students, and a variety of other activities. Depending upon the school system, supplemental pay may be provided for activities that require an abundance of time, but that is not a hard-and-fast rule. Many teachers find themselves working several nights a week on extracurricular activities. Try to find activities that correspond with your interests, which will make participation more enjoyable for you.

When to Say Yes and When to Say No

"While it is important to take an active role in professional organizations and to be a member of the various educational committees, teachers must be careful not to over-extend themselves to the point that they have no time to prepare themselves for what is really important—planning and teaching in the classroom."

—Janice Hogan, Principal

Learning to say no can be a difficult thing, especially when a teacher is in a new job and is eager to please. It is important, however, to recognize that no one person can do all that needs to be done. The more one is willing to do, the more that person is asked to do. So it becomes necessary to think things through and prioritize the demands of your job. You must continually ask yourself what your purpose is. As has been discussed, you will have to do some things that do not appear to have anything to do with teaching. These may be things that your administrator or school board require, thus becoming part of the job. If what you are being asked to do is not a job requirement, ask for time to make a decision. Think about your priorities and interests, talk to your mentor or colleagues, and determine if it will be a practical fit with your other responsibilities. There may be times when you need to accept a responsibility simply because it is your turn. You will have some choices, and you must recognize the difference between the times when it is appropriate to say no and when it is not.

PROFESSIONAL DEVELOPMENT

Teachers are provided ample opportunities to learn new concepts, methods, and approaches through professional development. You will not only be encouraged to take advantage of the classes, workshops, or conferences offered, but in some cases you will be required to do so. Though you may tire of continuing your education, remember that this training will help you to become better at what you do.

Lifelong Learning

"Being a professional means having a love for learning—always learning new methods, practices, and strategies to make learning interesting."

—Renee Bass, Teacher

One of the reasons teachers become teachers is because they love to learn. Learning keeps teachers up to date in the classroom. That is why most school districts allow teachers one or two professional days each year to attend conferences or workshops. Working closely with other teachers is also an effective way to stay current. Burke (2000) believes it is important to "seek like minds who are committed to learning and who are interested in discussing what we learn" (p. 9). You will learn from your colleagues; you will learn from professional development; you will learn from your students. As teacher Cindy Delcour says, "As long as you are teaching, you are learning."

Contributing to the Community of Learners

"Learning communities create 'spaces' for teachers to form professional relationships, to share information, and to provide collegial support" (Phillips, 2003).

Veteran teachers will all agree on one thing: Education cycles. Terminology and programs may change from one decade to the next. Even ideas may come and go. But the goals of education throughout the generations stay very much the same—preparing students to become lifelong learners and successful in their world.

Richard DuFour (2004), educator and author, refers to the cycle of "reform efforts" in education when he says,

> In this all-too-familiar cycle, initial enthusiasm gives way to confusion about the fundamental concepts driving the initiative, followed by inevitable implementation problems, the conclusion that the reform has failed to bring about the desired results, abandonment of the reform, and the launch of a new search for the next promising initiative. (p. 6)

In past years, numerous concepts have become trends. Educators who stay in the profession for any length of time must learn to adapt, take the good, throw out the ineffective, and build upon the foundation of what works.

When decisions are made in school systems, it is often the administration or the school board who makes them, causing teachers to feel they have little input or impact upon the solutions to problems that are very real to them. Teachers may feel that the general public or even their own school systems do not consider them professionals for a variety of reasons. Schools have experienced success when teachers take ownership of some of the decision-making and feel empowered to make a difference in their own educational world.

An example of a successful program was developed a number of years ago by DuFour when, as a principal, he began working in his school on teacher empowerment. Over a period of years, Adlai Stevenson High School in Chicago became one of the most acclaimed schools in the nation. DuFour began training other schools in this area of teacher empowerment and solving problems, and Professional Learning Communities were born. DuFour (2004) believes that every professional in the learning community should consistently focus on the following three questions:

- What do we want each student to learn?

- How will we know when each student has learned it?
- How will we respond when a student experiences difficulty in learning? (p. 9)

Teacher Shannon Cuff was sent by her high school in Willard, Missouri, to the training offered by DuFour. She became a coach for the rest of the school faculty and said, "It wasn't until we became a Professional Leaning Community that teachers felt empowered enough to work toward changes." She noted that for the process to work, the principal must be on board and trust the staff enough to be a part of the decision-making process. According to Cuff, one of the components that makes the Professional Learning Community work is a steering committee, composed of selected faculty, school board members, students, parents, and administrators.

Most schools have some sort of a vision or a mission statement and train their teachers to work toward this goal, whether they have adopted a particular model such as DuFour's Professional Learning Community or their own particular plan. Your role as a professional is to find your place, your niche, within the community. The way to do this is to follow your strengths. What role in a group do you like to play? For example, if you are a leader, then you might volunteer to be one of the teachers in your school who goes for specific training. If you are detail-oriented and like to make plans, you could volunteer to schedule meetings. You will gain more personal and professional satisfaction and reward if you find your place within your community of learners.

Inservice Workshops

"The majority of the learning from inservice workshops occurs when teachers apply what they learned in their own classrooms."
                    —Jana Loge, Missouri Reading Initiative District Trainer

While you are in school working on your teaching degree, you are referred to as a preservice teacher, but before you know it, you will officially be an inservice teacher. The purpose of inservice workshops is to help teachers learn new teaching methods, strategies, and information. Many schools provide several of these workshops a year.

On those days, school usually will be dismissed early or for the entire day so that teachers can attend these sessions.

Topics for workshops are widely varied. Many times administrators send out surveys to teachers asking for suggestions for workshop training. If your school is open to suggestions, offer ideas that you think might help you. To determine what types of workshops you could use, think about areas in your classroom where you struggle. For example, if you teach high school history and you notice your students are struggling with the readings, you might request a workshop on content area reading strategies that will help students get meaning from what they read. Or if you are having problems motivating your students, request a speaker who specializes in that area.

Obviously, not every workshop that you are required to attend will be of interest to you. Whether you want to be there or not, it is imperative that you listen, pay attention, participate actively, and act like a professional. You will be surprised that teachers at these meetings often act in ways they would never allow their students to act. Teachers are notorious for talking during meetings. Don't be like that. Be the professional you are expected to be.

Professional Organizations and Conferences

"In order to grow professionally, it is important for teachers to participate in their professional organizations."
—Janice Hogan, Principal

*B*eing an active member in professional organizations is an excellent way to stay up to date in your field. Most fields of study have their own organizations. Many reading teachers belong to the International Reading Association (IRA). English teachers may join the National Council for Teachers of English (NCTE). There are similar organizations for all subjects, including math, music, science, and technology. See the Internet Resources section of this book for a list of web sites for professional organizations for each subject area.

Other organizations span the curriculum for all teachers, such as the National Education Association (NEA) and state organizations such as the Missouri State Teachers Association (MSTA). All of these organizations offer conferences that last anywhere from one day to one week. Most organizations also publish one or more journals or magazines. Both the conferences and journals are designed to inform teachers of current research relating to their respective fields and to help them implement new teaching ideas or strategies. An advantage of membership in some of these organizations is that they offer liability insurance for you as a teacher as well as support and assistance with problems you may have such as unjust accusations or discrimination. When you begin a teaching job, ask teachers in your building or district what organizations they belong to and ask for information regarding these to help you decide which would be the best fit for you.

If you are not already a member of a professional organization, now is a good time to become involved. Find out from your college professors what organizations you should join. One of the advantages of joining as a student is that you will be able to get reduced membership rates.

Most schools provide teachers with one or two days specifically designed for professional development. These days are not sick days and cannot be used for any purpose other than professional development. Generally, you may choose which conference you would most like to attend. However, administrators may occasionally request that you attend a certain conference. For example, if you are a junior high teacher in a district that is considering a change to the middle school concept, you may be asked to attend a middle school conference and then come back to report to the other teachers. Or your administrator may send you to a middle school that is grounded in the middle school concept to observe and relate your findings to your faculty or middle school committee. If you are specifically asked to attend but you don't really wish to, the professional thing to do is to go anyway unless you have a strong, legitimate reason that you can't.

Many times, organizations will hold their conferences in interesting places near entertainment centers such as Disneyland in order to attract more members. While it is wonderful to plan outings during the evenings to see the sights, be sure to attend as many workshops as you can. Remember, you are there to learn.

Graduate Courses

"I especially liked my graduate courses in the reading department because I learned practical skills like how to give various reading assessments and how to teach strategies for reading in specific content areas. Some teachers don't realize how reading affects every subject."
—Russell Cox, Teacher

While it is a good idea to begin working on your master's degree early in your teaching career, it might also be smart not to take graduate classes your first year of teaching. You will be busy learning the ropes as a first-year teacher. As soon as you feel you can handle it, start slowly by taking an occasional course. Taking graduate courses while you are teaching can help you stay current with what is going on in your profession. It will also provide you with opportunities to see and interact with other teachers outside of school. Many teachers find graduate school much more meaningful than their undergraduate studies because they are able to immediately put into practice what they are learning in their classes. For example, what they learned in class on Monday night, they can try out with their students on Tuesday.

When choosing which courses to take or in what area to specialize for your master's degree, think about your own interests and your desires or needs for further education. For example, an elementary teacher might want to work toward a master's in reading because teaching reading is one of the major responsibilities of an elementary teacher. You might also want to use the opportunity to get certified in another area, such as special education. Teacher Kerri Cox believes, "Taking graduate classes that could lead to a second teaching certificate is a great way to expand your opportunities in case you ever get tired of teaching the same subject every year."

Not only will graduate classes increase your knowledge, but they will most likely also increase your income. Most schools have a salary schedule that provides regular increments in salary with additional college credits.

Teacher Study Groups and Support Groups

"Educators need to work with each other to think, analyze, and create conditions for change within their specific circumstances that relate to their personal or professional needs" (Short, Giorgis, & Pritchard, 1993).

Teacher study groups and teacher support groups can offer you a place to continue learning and growing. A teacher study group is defined as "a collaborative group organized and sustained by teachers to help them strengthen their professional development in areas of common interest" (Cramer, Hurst, & Wilson, 1996, p. 7). In these groups, teachers work on individual and group goals together. According to Bullough and Gitlin (1991), teachers need to be a community of learners supporting and sustaining each other's growth.

Teacher study groups are a great place to meet with other teachers with the sole purpose of sharing and learning new ideas. The study groups can revolve around a book study, a topic, a closer examination of student work, or anything that the teachers want to learn more about. For example, teachers in one school formed a group to study the book *Teaching with Love and Logic,* by Jim Fay and David Funk, because they were struggling with disciplinary issues.

Teacher support groups differ from study groups in that their purpose is less for study and more for the affective side of teaching. The purpose of a teacher support group is to help teachers deal with the more personal and stressful situations they face such as dealing with a difficult student, parent, or administrator or feeling the effects of teacher burnout and teacher isolation. Support groups will most likely emphasize emotional growth and problem solving. Sometimes teachers just need to talk with other teachers. At one school, teachers set aside one night a month to go out for an early dinner. It may seem odd that you can teach right across the hall from someone and still never have a chance to talk, but that's how it often works.

If your school does not already have a teacher study group or support group in place, do not hesitate to start one. Ask other teachers if they might be interested in meeting weekly or monthly.

Professional Development Plans

"When it comes to the education of our children, nothing matters more than the knowledge, skills and attitudes of their teachers" (Urbanski & O'Connell, 2004).

Part of being a professional is being intentional about setting goals to continue your educational growth and development. Recognize that you will need a plan for staying current with new research in education, continuing to hone your teaching skills, and staying motivated through professional development. Many school districts will want your plan on paper. Some will expect a plan each year, while others may ask you to prepare a five-year plan. In these plans you will outline what goals you want to achieve and list specific ways you plan to reach these goals.

If you are receiving a teaching degree from a state that no longer offers a lifetime teaching certificate, then you will probably be required to establish a professional development plan with your state in order to keep your teaching certificate current. If you don't do what the state requires of you, you can lose your certification. Now is the time to find out what is required in your state. Write it down. Make a checklist. Keeping your state teaching certificate current is solely your responsibility, and not a task to take lightly. Your professors and advisors work closely with your state's department of education and should be able to provide you with the necessary information.

When you are new to a school district, you will most likely be assigned a mentor who will work with you as you develop your professional development plans. If one is not assigned to you, ask your principal about your responsibilities in this area.

Professional Teaching Portfolios

"Professional teaching portfolios offer teachers the opportunity to show not only their teaching strengths but also their heart and soul and passion for teaching" (Cramer, Hurst, & Wilson, 1998, p. 578).

Professional teaching portfolios are "an organized collection of documents, letters, papers, and pictures that lauds your personal and professional achievements in a compact, concrete way" (Cook & Kessler, 1993, p. 15). Preparing a portfolio is an excellent way to showcase yourself as a professional. From as far back as Rembrandt, portfolios have been used to highlight work for people in professions such as art, photography, and architecture.

You may be in a school system that requires its teachers to compile teaching portfolios linked to teaching standards as part of their teacher evaluation system or for state accreditation purposes. You typically will be given guidelines and suggestions as to the types of things to include in the teaching portfolio. Additionally, some schools require departmental portfolios, including common assessments, projects, or assignments. In this situation, you would work with other teachers to compile the components of the portfolio. Determining the skills you expect your students to master and how you will assess those skills is a vital part of your teaching. Working with other teachers to create common assessments will strengthen the consistency of your program and better prepare your students. Working together as a team is essential for teachers who care about what is best for their students and their schools.

E-portfolios have become popular in the past several years. These are compiled on a disk to share with a prospective principal on a job interview or are posted on your own web site. By preparing an

e-portfolio, you are not only highlighting your accomplishments as a teacher, but you are also demonstrating your technological expertise.

Whether your professional teaching portfolio is compiled in a notebook or electronically, some types of items to include are:

- Cover letter

- Resume

- College transcript

- Letters of recommendation

- Philosophy of education

- Evaluations from student teaching or practicums

- Sample lesson plans

- Samples of work such as thematic units from your college classes

- Samples of student work

- Pictures of you working with students

What you choose to include is up to you, but remember to make it neat, organized, and professional, and remember the adage that sometimes "less is more." Including too much can be cumbersome for administrators to peruse; therefore, choose carefully and thoughtfully what to include.

PART FIVE

ADVICE FROM PROFESSIONALS

"Teaching is such a complex, intellectually stimulating profession that it's important to have the right combination of up-to-date resources and advice from experienced teachers" (National Teacher Recruitment Clearinghouse, 2004).

Principal, Emmett Sawyer:

"The role of teachers as professionals was redefined during the late 1990s. The two issues that caused this redefinition are school funding and accountability. School funding issues have caused a wide array of individuals, from legislators to parents, to view outcomes of school systems in terms of cost benefit analysis. The funding issues have influenced the consumers of school systems to demand accountability. Teacher quality is a major issue of the No Child Left Behind Legislation of 2001. The power of the microscope has increased exponentially. What does this mean for teachers? How do teachers remain professionals when they are viewed and feel more like factory line workers? My experience leads me to believe that if teachers consider and practice three critical components, they will be perceived as professionals by the public. These three critical components are teachers' knowledge and skill base, reflective practice, and systems thinking.

More than ever before, teachers need a deep knowledge and skill base to be effective with students engaged in the teaching/learning process and to communicate appropriately with parents. The variables that negatively impact student learning (e.g., poverty) appear to be increasing in many school districts. For example, in one large district in my area, students eligible for free and reduced lunch is increasing at a rate of 1% per year. At the same time, more students with special needs are being included in regular classrooms rather than being served in alternative settings. Teachers must have a deep knowledge and skill base to serve students with a wide range of learning and social needs and be able to communicate those needs to parents. Statements by teachers to parents such as, 'Mark just needs to work harder,' or 'Don't worry, Mary will be okay,' will not suffice any

72

more. Parents want more sophisticated answers that demonstrate that the teacher as a professional knows why the problem exists and what strategy is appropriate to address the problem.

Reflective practice holds great promise for improving instruction, which will affect how the teacher is viewed as a professional. Who better to evaluate the application of theory, knowledge, and skills in the classroom than the practitioner who is applying them? Who better to determine appropriate rates of student progress based on curriculum, instruction, and assessment than the classroom teacher? Who knows better where one needs to improve than a teacher reflectively evaluating his/her classroom performance? The reflective practitioner operates at a higher plane in the classroom that is more professional than the teacher who practices a recipe approach to teaching.

While space does not permit a discussion of Peter Senge's five disciplines in his book, *The Fifth Discipline Fieldbook* (1994), one discipline, systems thinking, is crucial for teachers to understand and practice in this age of accountability. Teachers must realize that what they think and how they behave in the classroom with even one student affects the organization or system. It determines the effectiveness of the system. When teachers practice systems thinking, the isolationism of teachers that is so pervasive in schools will disappear and more effective solutions to problems will be discovered and implemented. Furthermore, teachers will usurp the responsibility for accountability away from those outside the system and place it in the hands of those who can really make effective and substantive change.

Teachers must take control of their destiny by holding themselves accountable and solving their own problems. By developing a deep knowledge and skill base that leads to reflective practice founded in systems thinking, teachers will no longer be viewed as amateurs; rather they will be viewed as professionals adding value to their communities."

Principal, Janice Hogan:

"Teachers are professionals, and they should act and be treated as such. I know of few, if any, professional people who have a greater responsibility and task than teachers. Teachers should never, ever lose sight of the tremendous responsibility they are given in the educating of our children.

Teachers are different than many professionals in that they can never leave their role as teachers. In fact, if they try to take on another role with their students, it will lead to trouble every time. An example of this is trying to be a buddy or best friend with the students. When the students see the teacher in any role other than as teacher, the students become confused about what is also acceptable behavior for them in the classroom.

I believe it is important for teachers to look professional in their appearance and dress. It should go without saying that we as educators need to be neat and clean. Further, you should be able to tell the teachers apart from the students or the custodian. From my perspective as an administrator, there is certainly a difference in how students act and respond to the teacher based on the teacher's appearance. It's the same concept we observe in student behavior when they are required to dress up for a performance or other school activity. When teachers consistently dress down, it makes a difference in their students' behavior and how they interact with that teacher.

In order to grow professionally, it is important for teachers to participate in their professional organizations. When new teachers come into a school system they need to be active in their local teacher organization, committees, and so on. A word of caution is also necessary here. While it is important to take an active role in professional organizations and to be a member of the various educational committees, teachers must be careful not to over-extend themselves to the point that they have no time to prepare themselves for what is really important—planning and teaching in the classroom. I'm afraid that in education today, teachers are too overloaded with non-teaching duties that inevitably can have a detrimental effect in the classroom.

Teachers need to be prepared *every* time they enter the classroom. Just as you would not want your surgeon to enter the operating room and 'fly by the seat of his pants,' you should not enter the classroom unprepared. A teacher should over-plan, not under-plan. Lesson plans should be detailed enough so that not only the teacher himself can follow them, but also the administrator or substitute teacher can understand the objectives and activities for the lesson. As a professional, the teacher must cover his or her bases as much as possible in an absence. Alternative lesson plans need to be made available to the principal in case something unexpected happens to ensure that learning continues to occur in the classroom. It is very upsetting to me when the teacher leaves his class, a substitute, and an administrator in a lurch by assigning an entertaining video or a study hall for his students.

Along the same lines, it is unprofessional for teachers to spend an inordinate amount of time on things that do not contribute to the objectives of the course. Recently, I saw on one teacher's lesson plans that he was showing a historical movie, which took two weeks of this particular class period for the students to view. This movie had no direct relationship to the content matter of the class. While it may be true that there could be an educationally sound reason for showing that particular film in some situations, when I asked this teacher for his justification, he stated that it was because his students had been working hard and he wanted to give them a break. This is the most unprofessional response I can think of. He spent four class periods showing a movie unrelated to the subject matter to give the *students* a break. This teacher did not realize the importance of teaching and his responsibility for student learning.

A teacher as well as the principal will deal with discipline problems when the teacher allows students to be off-task in the classroom. Not all discipline matters are a result of students being off-task in the classroom, but I can tell you as an administrator that if you have unprepared classroom teachers, you will have to deal with many more discipline issues.

Sometimes because we as teachers are human, we don't always handle situations in a professional manner, but it is very important for us to try to do so. In dealing with an unruly student or angry parent, if we respond in a hateful, sarcastic, or cutting manner, our success will be jeopardized.

The faculty workroom should be a place where teachers can share. This sharing should be of a positive nature. It should never be a place where teachers tear down their pupils, each other, or the administration. Many times in a school system, as with any organization, decisions are made in which everyone is not in agreement. However, once decisions are made, all staff members need to abide by them. Faculty workrooms can be a place where discontent, negativism, and backbiting flourish. This will not happen if all staff members act in a professional manner.

It is equally important that teachers not allow students to complain and discuss other staff members in their classrooms. Professionalism involves not only what you say and do, but also what you allow or don't allow to be said or done in your classroom.

Good attendance is an important part of professionalism. When a teacher is not in his or her classroom, it is not the same as when a cashier does not show up for work. Even with the best of substitute teachers, the same level of learning does not occur when the regular classroom teacher is absent. Just because we have ten sick days doesn't mean we have to use them. They are there if they are needed, but are not to be taken advantage of. Teachers need to realize that what we do is too important, too significant, for others just to fill in. When the teacher is absent from the classroom, the students lose out."

Principal, Randall Wallace:

"Teaching is a demanding profession. As professionals, teachers must frequently resolve complex, school-related issues. The following situations describe how the personal inclinations of two beginning teachers interfered with their decision-making. These teachers reacted to classroom issues on an emotional level rather than relying on knowledge and information they should have acquired from their professional training.

A few years ago, I received a call from a teacher, Mrs. Driscoll, who asked if she could visit with me. She wanted to discuss her first year of teaching with someone outside of her school community and thought that I might have some insights about why her contract was not renewed. As we talked, I realized the focus of her dismissal centered on her teaching of reading.

Mrs. Driscoll had an excellent understanding of reading based on holistic theory. She was passionate and enthusiastic about teaching reading from this perspective. However, she was hired to teach first grade in a school where teaching from a skill-based, basal series was expected. The second-grade teacher assumed Mrs. Driscoll would follow the format of the basal series so that a smoother transition would occur when first-grade students advanced into the second-grade reading program. Furthermore, an accreditation team had recently visited the school where the principal and faculty had to verify how students were monitored as they progressed throughout the grades. The basal chapter and unit tests were offered to the accreditation team as a consistent, inter-grade form of accountability. Regarding Mrs. Driscoll's situation, the principal expressed concern that if every teacher taught reading based upon different teaching methods, it would be difficult for the school to demonstrate the year-to-year growth of students. And, finally, parents were supportive of the basal reading program because it was associated with a school history of generating large numbers of outstanding graduates. Yet, the basal approach did not correspond with Mrs. Driscoll's child-centered, strategy-based reading philosophy, and she was unwilling to align her reading program to fit more closely with the school's curriculum.

While Mrs. Driscoll's adherence to her reading philosophy might be seen as a sign of personal strength, a teacher's professional responsibility extends beyond the classroom. Mrs. Driscoll did not meet the expectations of others in the school community. She did not understand that collaboration with other professionals was essential to the development of her students as they advanced beyond first grade. Had Mrs. Driscoll been willing to supplement the basal program with activities more in line with her philosophical beliefs, she may have eventually moved others into seeing the strengths of her approach and ultimately changed the reading curriculum. Along with addressing the needs of their students, professional teachers know that reading is a collaborative venture that takes into account the goals of the school, thoughts of other teachers, and concerns of parents.

Mr. Hascall began his teaching career seeking to be well-liked by all of his students, a desire of many beginning teachers. He faced the challenge of building meaningful relationships with older students. Older students reason and communicate much like adults, but often behave in ways that challenge teacher authority. Eventually, Mr. Hascall learned that a teacher's professional behavior lays the foundation for building positive teacher-student relationships.

Mr. Hascall's first teaching assignment was in grades six and seven. He was terminated before completing his second year of teaching. The erosion of classroom control and the loss of student respect likely started the first time a student approached him and pleaded for an extension of an assignment deadline. By granting the extension, Mr. Hascall thought he was establishing a positive, meaningful relationship with students. What he did not know was that from that point on other students would be expecting similar extensions. I became involved when parents and students came to me expressing concerns about favoritism and unfairness. Rules regarding assignment deadlines, for example, were not consistently enforced. Such inconsistency, justified by the teacher as reflecting compassion and understanding, created a classroom climate characterized by ambiguity and uncertainty.

Mr. Hascall also felt that he could befriend students if the classroom participated in making important classroom decisions. I remember walking into his classroom and saying to him that the seating arrangement needed to be changed to allow students an easier view of the white board and overhead screen. He explained to me that the class had played a major role in creating the seating arrangement and that he could not change it without creating a major disruption. It was at that point that I began to doubt Mr. Hascall's management skill and his ability to be an effective classroom leader. He did not understand that respect comes to teachers who clearly establish their authority and use that authority to administer academic policies and management procedures consistently. Students must develop a respect for their teachers based on professional behavior before sincere teacher-student friendships can be cultivated.

Mrs. Driscoll and Mr. Hascall were outstanding university students. In almost all respects, they acted professionally. However, when solving complex classroom problems, they let their personal attitudes, desires, and emotions affect the quality of their decisions. The demands on teachers are considerable. As professionals, teachers must apply the principles they learn in their preservice training, reflect on their previous teaching experiences, and be willing to seek advice and make changes when difficult decisions need to be made."

Principal, Carol Plumley:

"*A*ccording to a Webster's dictionary, a professional is one who conforms to the ethical standards of a profession. But in my opinion, the word *professional* evokes more meaning than just conforming to standards. Being a professional in education involves maintaining a careful balance of academic proficiency, an above average ability in interpersonal relations and communication, and an ability to have empathy for people.

I believe professionalism begins at the preservice level. Serious students of education turn into professional appearing and acting teachers. Teachers are definitely not created upon their graduation from college. Each is honed through dedication to rigorous study, careful preparation in related fields and a bit of idealism. I believe that all teachers should want to make a difference in our world.

Professionals set goals for themselves and their students. They know what they want to achieve. The intensity of their passion is evidenced through their creativity and desire to be successful with students. Parents are won over by teachers' concisely stated goals for the year and their ability to maintain the confidentiality of each student; and students see that their teacher is prepared to facilitate exciting lessons

79

that respect their learning styles and individual differences.

Education is so much more than bulletin boards and lesson plans, grading papers and decorating classrooms. Teachers are more like parents than ever as they teach children about right and wrong, conflict solving strategies, how to recognize propaganda, and tactful ways to be assertive with other students and adults. These professionals inspire students to want to achieve something special in their lives—to go out and make a difference just as they are doing.

During my tenure as an educator, I have experienced the deaths of students and fellow teachers. I have comforted children who have lost grandparents and pets. I have been spat upon and kicked. I have been threatened and called many names and have worked many eighteen-hour days, but I would not give up the sum of these experiences. A professional takes them all in stride and stays the course, focusing on what is best for children. Making a difference in our world for the next generation might not be everyone's mission, but I believe that it should be at the heart of every educator who 'conforms to the ethical standards of this profession.'"

Teacher, Jamie Combs:

"So many changes have taken place in education throughout my teaching career. As a veteran teacher of public education, I have witnessed some very trying times in the last decade. The biggest issue on most educators' minds these days is accountability. As I approach each new school year, I think of all the training the average teacher must now complete. To secure a teaching job, one must have completed at least a bachelor's of science degree in education, which entails four or more years of college. Missouri law does not certify teachers with a lifetime teaching certificate anymore (as was done when I graduated with my bachelor's degree in 1975); so recent graduates in teacher education programs must now complete their master's degree in so many years or their teaching certificate will be revoked. I currently teach in a school system that also requires several hours of professional development each year.

I don't remember having to attend hours and hours of extra training and professional development when I first started teaching, but in the past seven years, I have received more inservice training and professional development than I have had in my entire teaching career. I am just now completing my master's degree in reading after almost twenty-five years of teaching experience. What has taken me on this journey so late in my career? Accountability! Even veteran teachers are on edge about the issue of accountability. My school was labeled a 'failing school' because we didn't make adequate yearly progress in both reading and math on our state tests. Our school's faculty had extra training, meetings, walk-through evaluations, and close scrutiny by experts in the field of education.

All of this has led me to evaluate my own professional ability. Am I worthy of doing my very best to make all students successful? As I began teaching full time again, after a leave of absence to raise my own children, I came back to my career with a new and refreshed outlook. I knew that education was again taking a new direction and that I needed to learn so much more. I wasn't really into the computer age of learning, or cooperative learning, or facilitating learning. I discovered that I needed to be trained and get with the new age of teaching. One can get stuck in the easy way out and go with the old comfortable ways of traditional teaching, or get excited about all of the *new* ideas in education. I chose to become excited!

I have found that I need to know more about teaching on a daily basis. I'm not too old to learn new ideas and strategies. Valuable training can help me do more for my students. I need to be the best I can be, so they can be the best they can be. Accountability does have its positive aspects. My advice to the new teacher is to never quit being a student."

Teacher, Patsy Bowser:

"In my years of teaching there are several hints I have learned that I would pass on to new teachers to help them learn what it means to be a professional.

- *Establish a time management program so that your entire life is not consumed with teaching.* Some tasks must be accomplished, while others can slide. Do the tasks that must be done first so that you can prioritize the rest. You can't do everything. You don't have to be perfect.

- *Know yourself.* Don't allow others to set your course for you. Always maintain a sense of humor and see the lighter side of as many situations as possible. Learn to laugh at yourself; it's good therapy.

- *Children want boundaries.* They will push to the limit to see if you will back down from the boundaries you've set. Therefore, you must be prepared to enforce the consequences you have set when your students go beyond the boundaries set for them. If children see that you will back down or waiver from what you have said, they will make your life miserable. They will forever see just how far they can go.

- *Be fair!* If children realize that you are fair, they will respect that. The rules must apply to everyone equally. When they don't, children resent it. When you have lost your credibility with them, a school year can seem like an eternity.

- *Treat your students with respect and courtesy.* Model a caring yet firm role in their lives. Allow them to see that we all make mistakes, and growing from those mistakes is what helps us to become caring, responsible citizens.

- *The teacher's workroom is just that—a workroom.* It is a place to make copies, make phone calls, or do other necessary tasks that must be a part of your day's work. It is also a place where you can create myriad troubles for yourself. A school is an example of our society; therefore, you will find the same kinds of problems in your school as you do in our world—cliques form, people belittle each other, personalities clash, and there are always some who do not want to pull their fair share of the load. The secret to not getting caught up in all these dramas is to maintain your professionalism. Teaching is a professional occupation, and we must be above all of the pettiness found in our society. Focus on what your real job is, which is to train and educate young people for the future. It is a daunting responsibility! There is no time in this profession to tear each other or our children down. We are their role models. For some of our students we may be the only positive influence in their lives. We must make sure we hold that responsibility as a high priority each day. Teaching is a calling; it is not a job. We do touch many lives each day. We must be ready for the test.

- *Make sure you treat yourself well.* Eat healthily and get plenty of rest because each day will require you to be alert and positive. Take time away from school to do things you enjoy. This allows you to replenish yourself so that you don't resent the emotional toll each day demands.

- *Parent conferences can be a scary part of your new job. Remember to set limits with the parents as well as with your students.* Establish a time limit per conference; have notes jotted down about each student that you want to cover; don't get into personalities with parents; keep the focus on the priority you have set for each individual conference; maintain your professionalism; don't discuss other students and their problems; and let parents see that you care about their child. Treat each parent with dignity and respect; treat them like you want your child's teacher to treat you.

- *Make friends* with the custodians, cooks, and secretaries; they can make your life much easier because they are really the ones who run the school."

Teacher, Gina Cowin:

"*A*s a preservice teacher I was terrified by the responsibility and the obligation of being a teacher. All of those minds relying on me. All of those administrators, parents, and students depending on me. Was I qualified? I sure didn't feel like it.

I hadn't even finished my undergraduate degree when I enrolled in graduate school. In a continuing search for learning that would help me to help my students, I stayed in school even while I was teaching, eventually receiving a master's, specialist's, and Ph.D. I learned new methods, new philosophies, new approaches.

The formal education plus each year of classroom experiences has taught me many things. In the last 31 years I've taught sixth, fifth, third, and second graders, undergraduates, and graduates. I still feel the weight of responsibility and obligation to each and every student. But all of the best intentions in the world won't make a good teacher. It also takes a lot of organization, hard work, creativity, and persistence. Even more essential are a sense of humor and a genuine love of children. If you can say yes to these characteristics, then you just might have what it takes.

There are some steps that I've found make the whole teaching process a lot easier. This following list is what I've learned about the importance of professionalism in teaching.

- *Begin by establishing a rapport with your students and their parents.* I send a newsletter to parents before I ever meet my students. I introduce myself with a short personal and professional biography. I include sayings, poems, pictures, and an invitation for both students and parents to become active members of our class. I explain my teaching philosophy and techniques, talk about general developmental stages for the grade I'm teaching, establish basic classroom rules, and explain my discipline policy. If you decide to use this idea, be sure all of your rules and policies are in agreement with established policy in your school and district. Before mailing your letter to parents, give a copy to your principal and ask him or her to read it and provide feedback if necessary. Keeping your principal, parents, and students informed will keep your headaches to a minimum. I also send a weekly update to parents with an extra copy for my principal.

- *Be organized!* Establish a routine in your classroom that works for you and the children. It takes a lot of pre-organizing, trial-and-error, or, better yet, trial-and-success. A well-organized room is easy to explain, and within a few days the children can handle many of the daily tasks. This builds their responsibility and reliability and makes life much easier for you.

- *Once classes start, get to know your students as real people and allow them to know you, too.* Understanding who your students are will allow you to start from where they are. Use their prior knowledge as a foundation and then help them construct new knowledge and attain new heights.

- *Be consistent!* As you begin class, be sure to stick to your own rules. I try not to spend the first day listing rules, but discuss them as we move through the planned activities. Point out inappropriate behavior and let students know what consequences to expect. Students (children and adults) love to push the limits, but they also want someone to enforce those limits. They will be more likely to follow the rules if the rules are consistently enforced.

- *A word of caution—your students are individuals at different levels of maturity, intellect, and motivation.* Learn not to make too many rules and don't make mountains out of molehills. General rules for order and cooperation are needed. Teaching children about actions and consequences—both good and bad—will give your students life skills that are invaluable to individuals and society.

- *Once you've established this comfort zone for students and parents, you can then challenge your students and open their minds to new worlds of learning and information.* Don't think everything will always run smoothly. Some days you'll go home drained and successful, other days you'll go home drained and discouraged, but for the time they're with you, your students deserve your full attention and positive efforts.

- ***Remember that kid logic is not adult logic.*** My third year of teaching one of my students used the word 'taught' in a sentence: 'I taught I saw a puddy cat.' I loved it and wrote on his paper, 'I did! I did see a puddy cat!' Did I lower his grade? Heavens no! How could I lower his grade when he had given me the best laugh I had had that week? Did I tell him how much I enjoyed his sentence? Yes. Did I explain the proper us of 'taught?' Of course. Did he and I learn something and have a good time doing it? Oh, yes indeed!

- ***Never forget that you must always be child-centered and a child advocate.*** I may not always be totally successful with each and every student, but I always know that I did my best, and that we have made some progress.

- ***Greg Denman, author and storyteller, says that 'if you want your students to be joyfully literate, you must be joyfully literate yourself.'*** This is a characteristic I try to model for all of my students. I can't think of a better goal than to inspire children to become joyfully literate.

This is what I have learned so far about being a teacher—a professional—and I'm still learning, every time I step into a classroom, every time I work with children."

Teacher, Kate Companik:

"As my students share and visit with me, I try to reflect upon my importance in their lives. The way I listen and talk with them is an important component of professionalism. I am a role model for these young people. I also believe it is important to share ideas and encourage my fellow teachers. We are a team working toward a common goal—teaching children."

Teacher, Barbara Carnagey:

"As a Title I teacher, I try to learn what is happening in education, especially in the field of reading. I want to know what is being discovered through research that will help me as I work with my students and their classroom teachers, and I want to share those ideas with my peers. In the past teachers have stayed in their classrooms, doing wonderful and creative things with their students, but too often have hoarded their ideas. Since the inception of 'inclusion' in the Title I program, I have learned so much from the classroom teachers that I now believe that every teacher should have the opportunity to visit other classrooms regularly. For me, professionalism means gladly sharing new ideas and knowledge with my fellow teachers."

Teacher, Lori Elliott:

"The first year of teaching is a mixed blessing. It is exciting and thrilling to finally put to practice all the wonderful theories learned in college. It is also frightening to realize that you are in charge of a diverse group of active learners. In order to survive this mixed bag of feelings and experiences, one must choose to be a 'pro.' Teaching is a serious calling and commitment. Professionalism is the key to success in the classroom as well as with parents, fellow teachers, and administrators. A first-year teaching pro realizes the following keys.

- *Teaching is a passion, not just an occupation.* There are no time clocks and fringe benefits in this profession. The work seems to never end. The changes never stop. However, the treasure is found in the students and the connections made with them. This passion can only come from the heart, not a job description.

- *Teachers must be risk takers and forever students themselves.* No one 'arrives' in teaching. We are all learners. We always need to improve, regroup, and stay fresh. This requires time to read, explore, and discover. This involves taking risks. If we ask our students to be risk takers, so must we be willing to change and grow.

- *Teachers create the environment and climate of the classroom.* Teachers are the facilitators of learning. We set the tone for the classroom and behavior. If we choose to be loud and bossy, then our students will replay this modeling. We must create a positive classroom by being constantly aware of what we say and do and how we react and respond.

- *Teachers must stay true to themselves and their students.* We all have different personalities and teaching styles. There is no 'one way' to teach. We must know ourselves and stay true to our beliefs and thinking. However, in the process we must be willing to constantly scrutinize our methods and accept criticism and encouragement. We must be 'real.' Students can see through phonies and will take the opportunity to try and expose a 'fake.'

- *Teachers must dress for success.* People are judged by their covers. If we dress in a sloppy and unkempt manner, our students and parents will view us as unprofessional and slacking. We do need to dress for our teaching tasks, so suit and tie may not be appropriate. Yet, we should always be well-groomed and dressed in appropriate fashion. You never know when a superintendent or parent might show up at your door. Therefore, it is crucial to always look your best.

- *Teachers must set high expectations for themselves and their students.* We should be our own toughest critics. We must set goals for ourselves and constantly strive to meet high expectations. We must reflect on our teaching and interactions and try to improve regularly. We must set high standards for our students. Students will meet our expectations; thus, our standards must be great.

- *Teachers must stay clear of negative influences.* Positive people achieve greater rewards. Effective teachers must stay clear of negative teaching pitfalls such as the teacher workroom, after school gripe sessions, and sour groupings at faculty meetings. These environments breed negativity that will squash creativity and excitement. It is crucial to find a buddy or two who share your views and beliefs. Surround yourself with positive folks and you will reap the rewards of ingenuity and freedom. It is important to release feelings of frustration and anxiety. Just make sure you share with folks who can comfort and encourage you, not bring you further down in the process.

- *Teachers must be true to their personalities, yet always be prepared and organized for each day with students.* It is true that we are all different and have varying organizational strategies. This cannot be used as an excuse, however, for unprepared lessons and inefficient instructional time. The day will go more smoothly and more successfully when the teacher is organized and fully prepared. Learning is more connected and transitions are easier when the teacher has everything ready to go ahead of schedule.

- *Teachers must provide students with a literature-rich environment, filled with meaningful experiences in every subject area.* The world has changed in the last 20 years. Students are bombarded with stimuli on a constant basis. Our lifestyles move rapidly. Therefore, classrooms today must adapt to meet the needs of our students. Students need active, meaningful experiences to learn and process ideas. Literature and the arts should permeate classrooms. These activities are enriching and nourishing. Allowing students to move, participate in, and lead in their own learning will dispel discipline problems and negative attitudes.

- *Teachers must communicate with parents daily, weekly, and monthly for positive interactions and student growth.* Education is a community project. It takes parents, teachers, administrators, and students working together to see progress and growth. This means that parents must be constantly involved in communication about what goes on in the classroom. Teachers must open their doors to other teachers, administrators, and parents in order to provide positive interactions. Teaching is not a solo performance. Teaching is a musical production."

Teacher, Todd Varhalla:

"I remember my mentor, Dr. Lloyd Hervey, saying in a certification class, 'When you get in the classroom, you have to love the children. You can't like them. You like chicken and you eat it. You have to love the children.' We thought he was funny at the time with that comment, but after teaching for several years, I understand what he means.

Many of the students I teach come from poverty, and what I do daily in the classroom as far as self-esteem and praising these kids is broken down at home that evening. Students are constantly bombarded with messages by family and society that they are worthless. I teach language arts, but I usually try to model love and acceptance while maintaining high expectations for the students. I have had to understand that some of my students are coming from tough homes where parents don't always care, and the kids often lack basic skills you would think they should have. Teachers have to realize that with love and acceptance students will perform.

Just because students are in poverty does not mean they aren't smart. They are very smart, but the rules they know, the rules of poverty, do not apply to the rules in schools—schools function from a middle class mindset (Ruby Payne, *Understanding the Frameworks of Poverty*). We have to show students these rules and hope they have a desire to better themselves. As a teacher I want to give them more than they came with. For some, that is more knowledge, but for others, it is more love."

SUMMARY
KEYS TO BEING A PROFESSIONAL

- Practice good social skills.

- Know the expectations of your job and do them to the best of your ability.

- Prioritize your tasks and practice time management.

- Set goals for yourself and your students.

- Treat the student-parent relationship as confidential.

- Dress according to your school's standards.

- Be punctual.

- Be prepared.

- Know yourself so that you don't have to try to prove yourself.

- Communicate effectively, using correct speaking and writing skills.

- Establish strong relationships.

- Stay current in your field.

- Be a lifelong learner.

- Keep a positive attitude.

- Treat people with respect.

- Practice what you preach.

Teachers' ABC's of Professionalism

In an informal survey, teachers were asked to list one word that best describes their idea of a true professional. Here's their list.

Adaptable
Appearance (dresses professionally)
Approachable
Appropriate language
Articulate
Attends conferences
Attitude positive
Benevolent
Caring
Communication skills
Compassionate
Competent
Concerned
Considers all options
Consistent
Creative
Decision-making skills
Dedicated
Diligent
Does hands-on activities
Empathetic
Energetic
Engages in professional development
Enthusiastic
Fair
Flexible
Friendly
Genuine concern for students
Gives clear and precise directions for assignments
Good personality
Has time for student's questions
Helpful
High expectations
Intelligent
Interesting
Intuitive
Just

Keeps accurate records
Kind
Knowledgeable
Knows their content well
Lifelong learner
Listens
Loyal
Motivated
Motivational
Never stops learning
Nice
Organized
Patient
Positive
Prepared
Prioritizes
Punctual
Qualified
Reads
Reflective
Reliable
Resourceful
Respectful
Responsible
Sense of humor
Slow to anger
Steady
Strong beliefs
Tactful
Unbiased
Values students
Well-spoken
Willing
Xerox expert
Yearn for excellence
Zealous

APPENDIX

A: Sample Elementary Weekly Letter to Parents
B: Sample Middle School Introductory Letter to Parents
C: Sample High School Letter to Parents: Goals and Skills
D: Sample Letter to Parents and Students
E: Sample Classroom Policy
F: Sample Classroom Rules
G: Sample Newsletter

APPENDIX A

SAMPLE ELEMENTARY WEEKLY LETTER TO PARENTS

September 15, 2005

Dear Parents,

Our year is off to a great start. I am enjoying getting to know your children. I plan to call everyone sometime this week just to touch base with you and see if you have any questions. If you do not have a phone, please send a note with your questions, and I will respond the following day.

We will have achievement testing during the mornings next week on Monday through Thursday. Please see that your children get a good night's sleep and eat a good breakfast.

We will have the first math chapter test on Friday. This chapter has covered place value, rounding, comparing and ordering numbers, counting change, and guess/check to problem solve. The students will have a review assignment on Thursday, which I will grade and send home Thursday night so they can review any problem areas with you.

Congratulations to four students who mastered the addition facts and to one student who mastered the multiplication facts. Students will continue taking the timed tests until they have mastered the facts. Please continue to have your child study at home.

We will also have a science test over Chapter 1 (pages A8-A33) over plants, their parts, and the life cycle this Friday. Your child has been given a study guide.

The school CARNIVAL is this Saturday from 2:00 to 6:00. We will have an old-fashioned cakewalk with cakes, pies, and cookies. The classes are competing to see who will have the most donated items. We are looking forward to an exciting day. Hope to see you there!

Have a great week,
Mrs. Companik

APPENDIX B

SAMPLE MIDDLE SCHOOL INTRODUCTORY LETTER TO PARENTS

August 14, 2005

Dear Parents and Students;

Welcome to Pleasant Hope Middle School! I am looking forward to working with you this year. Communication between parents, students, and teachers is essential for a good learning experience to take place. PLEASE contact me with any questions or concerns you have during the year.

Each student should have a folder and a spiral notebook to be used specifically for English class. Students also need a red pen or pencil to be used for corrections of daily work. Anything other than corrections should be completed in pencil or blue or black pen. All skills work assignments will be numbered and kept in the folder. Corrections will be made on each assignment. Any parent who wants to check his or her child's progress will be able to tell at a glance whether he/she is keeping up with the assignments. Additional hand-in assignments will be given for grades.

Students will be responsible for bringing their AGENDA to class daily and keeping assignments updated in it. Daily points will be given to each student for the completion and corrections of his/her work. Consistent attendance is important for mastery of the work. If a student misses class, it will be his/her responsibility to make up the missed work.

We will be spending a lot of time this year doing the Reading/Writing Workshop. Students will be reading books, writing in a reading log, and keeping records of their reading. Class time will be used for reading, but students will also need to spend much time at home reading. Please encourage your child to read. We will also be doing lots of writing. Students will write many pieces throughout the year. Again, I ask for your encouragement in this endeavor. The ability to read and write and a little "I want to" go a long way and will take your child anywhere he or she wants to go. By the way, if you have old books that would be appropriate for middle school level, and you want to get rid of them, please send them to school with your child. We can always use them!

I expect each student to behave in a responsible and respectful manner. Responsibilities go hand in hand with freedoms, and if students desire privileges, they must demonstrate their willingness to be cooperative in the classroom.

You may reach me before or after school through the school office. I welcome your communication. Please get in touch with me if you have a question or concern.

Thank you,

Mrs. Reding

Your child will get 10 points to begin the year if you sign below indicating you have read this letter.

Parent Signature _____

Student Signature _____

APPENDIX C

SAMPLE HIGH SCHOOL LETTER TO PARENTS: GOALS AND SKILLS

October 10, 2005

Dear Parents,

Your kids have so many talents; I am excited about the opportunity to help them develop their reading and writing skills. We have been doing lots of reading and basic skills work in English this first quarter. Your child should have been doing reading at home. We will continue with the reading workshop throughout the year and will be adding to it a writing workshop.

I want to take this time to explain some of the things we will be working on, so that you will better understand what your child is doing and what is expected of him/her.

- **Reading Skills:** As a class we will be working on comprehension skills: main idea, inference/drawing conclusions, cause/effect, fact/opinion.

- **Pleasure Reading:** The more your children read, the better they will become at it and the more successful they will be in all areas of school life and life after school. The annual state exams given have much reading on them; as your children become more comfortable with reading, they will be more efficient in taking the tests. All students are expected to be continually reading a book for pleasure. Reading for enjoyment will help your child become a better reader.

- **Writing Skills:** Students are expected to write in complete sentences, using appropriate punctuation, spelling, and proper usage. They will develop skills in revising and editing their writing. Students should be able to create a variety of writing passages, including personal experience narratives, descriptive passages, persuasive essays, various types of poetry, short stories, and responses to literature. Writing will be kept in a portfolio.

- **<u>Literature</u>:** Students will identify euphemisms, loaded words, and figurative language. They will recognize literary techniques such as irony, plot, characterization, setting, theme, symbolism, stereotyping, flashback, story elements, author's purpose, and point of view.

- **<u>Library Skills</u>:** Students will be taken regularly to the library where, in addition to checking out books, they will be instructed in research skills and reference information.

I appreciate the support you give me—and your children. I know that you recognize that the time investment you make in them today will come back to you in many positive ways. Please encourage them in their schoolwork, and help them to know that they will benefit many times over for the effort they put into it now. Please feel free to contact me if you have any questions or concerns.

Thank you.

Mrs. Reding

APPENDIX D

SAMPLE LETTER TO PARENTS AND STUDENTS

August 22, 2005

Dear Parents and Students:

I want to welcome you to English Composition I and give you some information about the class. As you should be aware, taking this class gives students an opportunity for dual enrollment—both high school and college credit. Not all students will choose to receive college credit for the class; however, the class will be organized and run as a college class for all students, whether they are taking it for college credit or not. It is important for both students and parents to recognize that and be prepared for the standard of work that will be expected.

Composition I is just that—a composition class, which means there will be a great deal of writing required, including some intensive research and documentation. Please understand that simply showing up to class and completing in-class assignments will not guarantee a good grade. Outside work will be necessary and expected.

I have much experience in writing and in teaching, and I love being surrounded by students who have the desire to develop their talents and the tenacity to keep trying, even when it may be difficult. This will be a challenging class, but one that will stretch students, and I hope that it will even be a little bit fun!

I'm asking parents to sign below to let me know that you understand from the beginning that this is a class that would be equivalent to one in which your students might find themselves as college freshman. If you feel that your student has enrolled in this class without an understanding of the expectations, now would be the time to make some changes. Please contact me if you have any questions or concerns; I'll be more than happy to talk with you.

Thank you,
Mrs. Reding

Parent's Signature _____

APPENDIX E

SAMPLE CLASSROOM POLICY

CLASSROOM POLICY
7TH AND 8TH GRADE CORE CLASSES

CLASSROOM BEHAVIOR: Students are expected to be courteous and respectful to the teacher and their classmates. Conduct (including talking without permission) that interrupts the learning process will result in the following:
1. Warning
2. Isolation
3. Removal from the classroom
4. Conference with the principal and notification of parents

Certain types of behavior will automatically result in step 4 according to the severity and the reoccurrence of the behavior.

TARDIES: Being tardy is defined as NOT being seated in your appropriate seat when the bell has stopped ringing. Misconduct in the hall or classroom to avoid being tardy, such as running or shoving, will result in a tardy as well. A tardy is excused if, and only if, the office excuses it or a teacher issues a pass for the student.

A student's third tardy will result in being assigned to after school suspension.

GRADES: Quarter grades are assigned according to the following grading scale and are based on total points accumulated from projects, daily assignments, tests, quizzes, etc.
90-100% A; 80-89% B; 70-79% C; 60-69% D; and 0-59% F

Students will have some type of grade each day. If a student is absent, he or she will be held responsible for completing make-up work. Students will need to make arrangements with their teacher to make up any missed lab work or videos AFTER SCHOOL WITHIN ONE WEEK of the absence in order to receive credit for that activity.

ABSENCES: Almost all failing grades are the direct result of **poor attendance and/or failure to turn in work.** It is VERY IMPORTANT that you make every effort to be in class each time it meets and be sure ALL assignments are completed and TURNED IN!! Be sure you understand the attendance policy as outlined in the student handbook.

APPENDIX F

SAMPLE CLASSROOM RULES

CLASS RULES

BE PROMPT! All students are expected to be in class on time and to have assignments completed on time. This is a good habit to develop.

BE PREPARED! Students should bring all materials they might need to class as well as completed homework. Students are also expected to review for tests on their own prior to the test in class.

SHOW RESPECT! We have a zero tolerance policy for disrespectful comments and/or body language. All students are to be respectful to other students as well as their teachers and school property. This includes leaving personal property alone, keeping hands and feet to oneself, refraining from marking on school property, not interrupting when someone else is talking, etc. Earn respect from students and teachers by showing them respect!

BE RESPONSIBLE! Students are held accountable for their actions and may need to carefully consider the consequences of their actions.

DO YOUR BEST! It is impossible to raise a grade very much after a student has neglected to do assignments well or has received zeros for assignments he or she failed to do.

We are looking forward to a great year. Thank you.

Core teachers, 7th and 8th

Please sign and return this portion.

Student Signature_____

Parent Signature_____

APPENDIX G

SAMPLE NEWSLETTER

MRS. SMITH'S KINDERGARTEN CLASS NEWSLETTER
January 12-16, 2005

Bear Book Week

This week we are going to see how many books we can read about bears—real bears, stuffed bears, and even Berenstain Bear bears. Your child has been encouraged to look through your book collections at home and visit a library to find books about bears. We would also like to invite you to come read a book to our class about bears. On Friday afternoon, each student will do a bear book talk and show the class which of the books we read this week was their favorite.

Next Week's Letter of the Week: Q

As you go through your daily routine this week, take note of words your family sees and uses that begin with Q or have a Q in them. When in the car, look for words with the letter "Q" on billboards and signs. Talk about those words and what they mean. This will help your child make connections between letters, words, and how we use them.

Last Week's Letter of the Week: P

Our letter for last week was "P." Each student looked through the books we read and picked out one word that started with "P" to add to our word wall. Ask your child to show you which word he or she added to the list. See if your child can read the list of words aloud to you.

puppy	pony	pocket	popcorn
pumpkin	put	place	puffy
part	pick	plain	play
pull	pencil	pour	pat

INTERNET RESOURCES

Professional Education Organizations

American Federation of Teachers
http://www.aft.org/

Association for Supervision and Curriculum Development
http://www.ascd.org

National Middle School Association
http://www.nmsa.org

National Education Association
http://www.nea.org

Phi Delta Kappa
http://www.phideltakappa.com
National Education Fraternity

Professional Organizations for Teachers by Subject Area

American Association of Family and Consumer Sciences
http://www.aafcs.org

Association for Career and Technical Education
http://www.acteonline.org

Association for the Advancement of Computing in Education
http://www.aace.org

Council for Exceptional Children
http://www.cec.sped.org

Family and Consumer Sciences Education Organization
http://www.facse.org

International Reading Association
http://www.ira.org

International Society for Technology in Education
http://www.iste.org

International Technology Education Association
http://www.itea.org

Music Teachers National Association
http://www.mtna.org

National Association for the Education of Young Children
http://www.naeyc.org

National Art Education Association
http://www.naea-reston.org

National Business Education Association
http://www.nbea.org/

National Council of Teachers of English
http://www.ncte.org

National Council of Teachers of Mathematics
http://www.nctm.org

National Council for the Social Studies
http://www.socialstudies.org

National Science Teachers Association
http://www.nsta.org

Related Educational Links for Teachers

Educators' Reference Desk
http://www.eduref.org/

Education Week on the Web
http://www.edweek.org/

Education World: The Educator's Best Friend
   http://www.educationworld.com/a_curr/profdev061.shtml

Educational Testing Service
   http://www.ets.org

Eisenhower National Clearinghouse
   http://www.enc.org

Global Schoolhouse
   http://www.gsn.org

International Education and Resource Network
   http://www.igc.apc.org

MiddleWeb: Exploring Middle School Reform
   http://www.middleweb.com/

Newsbank, Information for teachers
   http://www.newsbank.com/

Praxis Information
   http://www.ets.org/praxis/index.html

Praxis: State-by-state requirements
   http://www.ets.org.praxis/prxstate.html

Public Broadcasting Service information and links for teachers
   http://www.pbs.org/teachersource/

Services for teachers
   http://www.teacher.com

State Departments of Education
   http://www.teacher.com/sdoe.htm
   Click on your state to find your state's Department
   of Education

United States Department of Education
   http://www.ed.gov

United States Department of Labor (teaching information)
   http://www.bls.gov/oco/ocos069.htm

Teacher Accreditation, Accountability, and Standards

Interstate New Teacher Assessment and Support Consortium
   Standards
   http://www.dpi.state.nc.us/pbl/pblintasc.htm

National Board for Professional Teaching Standards
   http://www.nbpts.org/

National Commission on Teaching and America's Future
   http://www.nctaf.org

National Partnership for Excellence and Accountability in Teaching
   http://ed-web3.educ.msu.edu/npeat/

National Teacher Accreditation
   http://www.ncate.org

Teacher Education Accreditation Council
   http://www.teac.org/about/index.asp

Teacher Recruitment

National Teacher Recruitment Clearinghouse
   http://www.recruitingteachers.org/channels/clearinghouse/

Recruiting New Teachers
   http://www.rnt.org

REFERENCES

Blake, S., Holcombe, L., & Foster, D. (1998). Technology and teachers: An investigation of attitudes and beliefs of introductory use by preservice teachers. Journal of Technology and Teacher Education, 6(1), 39-49.

Bullough, R., & Gitlin, A. (1991). Toward educative communities: Teacher education and the development of the reflective practitioner. In B. R. Tabachnick & K. Zeichner (Eds.), *Issues and practices in inquiry-oriented teacher education* (pp. 35-55). London: Falmer Press.

Bureau of Labor Statistics, United States Department of Labor. (2004). *Occupational outlook handbook, Teachers—Preschool, kindergarten, elementary, middle, and secondary.* Retrieved June 27, 2004 from http://www.bls.gov/oco/ocos069.htm

Burke, J. (2000). Teaching Sisyphus to juggle. *Educational Leadership, 57*(8), 8-12.

Carver, C. L. (2004). A lifeline for new teachers. *Educational Leadership, 61*(8), 58-61.

Cook, D., & Kessler, J. (1993, August). The professional teaching portfolio: A useful tool for an effective job search. *ASCUS Annual,* 15.

Cramer, G., Hurst, B., & Wilson, C. (1996). *Teacher study groups for professional development.* Phi Delta Kappan Fastback. Bloomington, Indiana: Phi Delta Kappa Educational Foundation.

DuFour, R. What is a 'Professional Learning Community'? *Educational Leadership, 61*(8), 6-11.

Glasser, W. (1993). *The quality school teacher.* New York: HarperCollins.

Graves, D. H. (2001). *The energy to teach.* Portsmouth, NH: Heinemann.

Hurst, B. (1998). Person working equals person learning. *Journal of Reading Education, 23*(3), 23-24.

Hurst, B. & Reding, G. (1999). *Keeping the light in your eyes: A guide to helping teachers discover, remember, relive, and rediscover the joy of teaching.* Scottsdale, AZ: Holcomb Hathaway.

Hurst, B., Wilson, C., & Cramer, G. (1998). Professional teaching portfolios: Tools for reflection, growth, and advancement. *Phi Delta Kappan, 79*(8), 578-582.

Interstate New Teacher Assessment and Support Consortium. (2004). *The INTASC Standards.* Retrieved July 3, 2004 from http://www.dpi.state.nc.us/pbl/pblintasc.htm

Keene, E. O., & Zimmermann, S. (1997). *Mosaic of thought: Teaching comprehension in a reader's workshop.* Portsmouth, NH: Heinemann.

Lawson, M. A. (2004). Leadership styles in secondary school science teachers. Unpublished doctoral dissertation, University of Missouri, Columbia.

Lee, J. O. (2003). Implementing high standards in urban schools: Problems and solutions. *Phi Delta Kappan, 84*(6), 449-455.

Lindsay, D. M. (1999). Effective communication or rude efficiencies? *American Secondary Education, 28*(1), 34-35.

National Board for Professional Teaching Standards. (2004). *What teachers should know and be able to do: The five core propositions of the National Board.* Retrieved July 3, 2004 from http://www.nbpts.org/about/coreprops.cfm

National Teacher Recruitment Clearinghouse. (2004). *Successful teaching.* Retrieved June 24, 2004 from http://www.recruitingteachers.org/channels/clearinghouse/successfulteacher/default.htm

Perrone, V. (1991). *A letter to teachers: Reflections on schooling and the art of teaching.* California: Jossey-Bass.

Phillips, J. (2003). Powerful learning: Creating learning communities in urban school reform. *Journal of Curriculum and Supervision, 18*(3), 240-258.

Posner, G. J., & Rudnitsky, A. N. (1994). *Course design: A guide to curriculum development for teachers.* New York: Longman.

Reding, G. (2002). The eMINTS Edge. *School & Community, 88*(4), 23-24.

Ritts, V., & Stein, J. R. (2004). *Six ways to improve your nonverbal communications.* Retrieved July 10, 2004 from http://honolulu.hawaii.edu/intranet/committees/FacDevCom/guidebk/teachtip/m-files/m-commu1.htm

Short, K. G., Giorgis, C., & Pritchard, T. G. (April, 1993). *Principal study groups and teacher study groups: An interactive and innovative approach to curriculum change.* Paper presented at the American Educational Research Association, 1993 Annual Meeting, Atlanta.

Smelser, N. J. (1998). Rules to serve by. *ASEE Prism, 8*(3), 32-35.

Toth, E. (1999). The Chronicle of Higher Education, Chronicle Careers. *Your first month in a new job.* Retrieved July 10, 2004 from http://chronicle.com/jobs/99/08/99082701c.htm

Tryneski, J. (1997). *Requirements for certification: Of teachers, counselors, librarians, administrators for elementary and secondary schools 1997-1998.* Chicago, IL: University of Chicago Press.

United States Department of Education. (2004). *Strategic goals.* Retrieved July 3, 2004 from http://www.ed.gov/about/reports/strat/plan2002-07/plan.doc

Urbanski, A., & O'Connell, C. (2003). *Transforming the profession of teaching: It starts at the beginning.* Paper commissioned for National Commission on Teaching and America's Future's National Summit on The First Three Years of Teaching. Retrieved July 10, 2004 from http://www.nctaf.org/article/index.php?g=0&c=3&sc=13&ssc=&a=39&navs=

Watts-Taffe, S., Gwinn, C. B., Johnson, J. R., & Horn, M. L. (2003). Preparing preservice teachers to integrate technology with the elementary literacy program. *Reading Teacher, 57*(2), 130-138.

Wesley, D. C. (2003). Nurturing the novices. *Phi Delta Kappan, 84*(6), 466-470.

Whole Child, The. (2004). *Establishing Strong Family-School Communication.* Retrieved July 11, 2004 from http://www.pbs.org/wholechild/providers/f-s.html

Williams, M. (1958). *The velveteen rabbit.* Garden City, NY: Doubleday & Company.

FURTHER READINGS

Boy, A., & Pine, G. (1971). *Expanding the self: Personal growth for teachers.* Dubuque, IA: Wm. Brown.

Brown, L. J., & Brown, J. R. (1992). Assessment of preservice elementary teacher education practices in parent-teacher conferencing. (ED35185).

Burbules, N. C. (1997). *Teaching and its predicaments.* Boulder, CO: Westview Press.

Canter, L. (1996). *The high performing teacher.* Santa Monica, CA: Lee Canter & Associates.

Collins, M. & Tamarkin, C. (1990). *Marva Collins' Way.* New York: J. P. Tarcher.

De Vries, M. A. (1991). *The complete word book: The practical guide to anything and everything you need to know about words and how to use them.* Upper Saddle River, NJ: Prentice Hall.

Duckworth, E. (1997). *Teacher to teacher: Learning from each other.* New York: Teachers College Press.

Fried, R. L. (1996). *The passionate teacher.* Boston: Beacon Press.

Hansen, D. T. (1995). *The call to teach.* New York: Teachers College Press.

Lawler, S. D. (1981). Effective parent-teacher conferences: A guide for student teachers. (ED313125)

Martin, J. M. (1992). Teachers' communication skills: The key to successful parent involvement. (ED348706)

McIntyre, D. J. (1996). *The reflective roles of the classroom teacher.* Belmont, CA: Wadsworth.

Morgan, A. L. (1989). Communication skills for teachers. (ED312729)

Packard, R. D. (1993). Professional teacher: Master communicator, researcher and scholar. (ED358053).

Palmer, D. J. (1998). *The courage to teach: Exploring the inner landscape of a teacher's life.* California: Jossey-Bass .

Piddocke, S., Magsino, R. F., & Manley-Casimir, M. E. (1997). *Teachers in trouble: An exploration of the normative character of teaching.* Toronto: University of Toronto Press.

Routman, R. (1991*). Invitations: Changing as teachers and learners K-12.* New Hampshire: Heinemann.

Shertzer, M. D. (1996). *The elements of grammar.* Macmillan.

Shull, I. D. (1998*). For the love of teaching: And other reasons teachers do what they do.* Acton, MA: VanderWyk & Burnham.

Strunk, W., & White, E. B. (1995). *Elements of style.* Needham Heights, MA: Allyn & Bacon.

Tryneski, J. (1997). *Requirements for certification: Of teachers, counselors, librarians, administrators for elementary and secondary schools 1997-1998.* Chicago, IL: University of Chicago Press.

Wakeford, M. E., & Williams, V. S. L. (1990). The use of communication skills and general knowledge scores for admission to teacher education programs: Policy recommendations. (ED336382).

Westheimer, J., & Cuban, L. (1998). *Among school teachers: Community, autonomy, and ideology in teachers' work.* New York: Teachers College Press.

Wong, H. K., & Wong, R. T. (2001). *The first days of school: How to be an effective teacher.* Mountain View, CA: Harry K. Wong Publications.

Woodward, P. (1997). *The teacher's almanac: The professional teacher's handbook.* Los Angeles, CA: Lowell House.

Youngs, B. B. (1993). *Enhancing the educator's self-esteem: It's your criteria #1.* Carson, CA: Jalmer Press.

INDEX

POSTSCRIPT

As we were completing the index for this second addition we realized that 19 times throughout the book we suggested that you "ask." An important part of being a professional is knowing enough to ask questions. It is your personal responsibility as a professional to learn all you can about your chosen profession. In their book *Mosaic of Thought,* Keene and Zimmerman (1997) state, "Of all qualities, questioning is fundamental to being human. It is how we dispel confusion, probe into new areas, strengthen our abilities to analyze and deduce" (99). It's part of being a professional.

One of the many conversations we had in the writing of this book was a story about two college students who had both failed to register for the same class. The class was closed, but both students needed the class to graduate. Both students sent an email message to the professor asking to be admitted to the class. One student explained the mix-up, apologized for any inconvenience it might have caused the professor, and humbly asked to be admitted into the class. The other student sent an email message demanding to be admitted into the class with an attitude that it was somehow the professor's fault the student didn't get in. One student acted in a very professional manner, while the other student did not.

Which student do you think got into the class? They both did. Because a professional treats all students the same, no matter what their social background or training. Some students have never been taught that there is a proper way to handle these types of situations. You will have these same students in your classroom. Some have been taught social skills and some have not. As a professional, you treat all students the same no matter what their social background and experiences.

On page 14 of this book we quote Wesley who said, "When veterans and novices work together in a nurturing relationship, each gets something of real value from the other. Veterans gain energy; novices gain inspiration." Thank you for the energy you have given us. We hope you have been inspired.

Beth Hurst and Ginny Reding